Nebraska
CURIOSITIES

Help Us Keep This Guide Up to Date

Every effort has been made by the authors and editors to make this guide as accurate and useful as possible. However, many things can change after a guide is published—establishments close, phone numbers change, facilities come under new management, and so forth.

We would love to hear from you concerning your experiences with this guide and how you feel it could be improved and kept up to date. While we may not be able to respond to all comments and suggestions, we'll take them to heart and we'll also make certain to share them with the authors. Please send your comments and suggestions to the following address:

Globe Pequot Press

Reader Response/Editorial Department

P.O. Box 480

Guilford, CT 06437

Or you may e-mail us at:

editorial@GlobePequot.com

Thanks for your input, and happy travels!

Curiosities Series

Nebraska
CURIOSITIES

Quirky characters,
roadside oddities &
other offbeat stuff

Rick Yoder and David Harding

Guilford, Connecticut

The prices, rates, and hours listed in this guidebook were confirmed at press time. We recommend, however, that you call establishments to obtain current information before traveling.

Copyright © 2010 by Morris Book Publishing, LLC

Photos by Rick Yoder and David Harding unless otherwise noted.
Maps by Tony Moore © Morris Book Publishing, LLC
Text design: Bret Kerr
Layout artist: Mary Ballachino
Project manager: John Burbidge

Library of Congress Cataloging-in-Publication Data

Yoder, Rick.
  Nebraska curiosities : quirky characters, roadside oddities & other offbeat stuff / Rick Yoder and David Harding.
      p. cm.
  Includes index.
  ISBN 978-0-7627-4683-5
  1. Nebraska—Guidebooks. 2. Nebraska—Description and travel. 3. Curiosities and wonders—Nebraska. 4. Nebraska—Miscellanea. I. Harding, David. II. Title.
  F664.3.Y63 2010
  978.2—dc22

                                                                    2009043092

Printed in the United States of America

10 9 8 7 6 5 4 3 2 1

To our wives, who were kind enough to let us go . . .
and smart enough to stay behind.

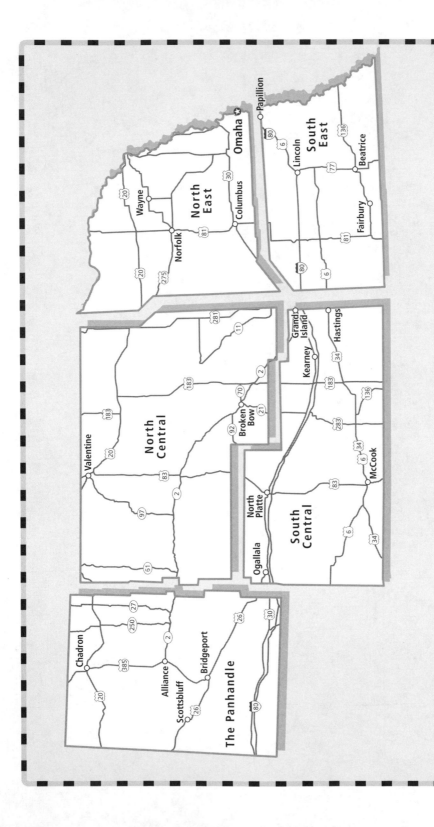

Nebraska Overview

contents

Acknowledgments   viii

Introduction   ix

CHAPTER ONE
Northeast   1

CHAPTER TWO
Lincoln and Omaha   45

CHAPTER THREE
Southeast   89

CHAPTER FOUR
South Central   131

CHAPTER FIVE
North Central   171

CHAPTER SIX
The Panhandle   205

Index   233

About the Authors   243

acknowledgments

We traveled the state in the hopes of finding all the curiosities known mostly to the locals. If it wasn't for the good advice and help from Nebraskans, Nebraskan-wannabes, and civic groups throughout the states, we'd have spent more time looking than finding. We humbly tender our thanks to those who took the time to talk to us and let us know of their local treasures, even though we weren't able to use every one: Carolyn Albracht, Patricia Barney, Dave Bartholet, Mike Boone, Mason Burbach, Janette Brungardt, Joe Clawson, Ms. Bernie Cunningham, Elizabeth Chase, Deb Crago, Julie Dickerson, Tina Domeier, Sue Dowse, Tony Dworak, Paul Eisloeffel, Mark Engler, Pepe Fierro, Wayne Fisher, Kim Grell, Peggy Haskell, Craig Henkel, Sheryl Hiatt, Gerald and Gloria Hilton, Gail Holmes, Kevin Howard, S. Horst, Cindy Howey, Dean Jacobs, Patrick Keough, Scott Knapp, Nancy Kratky, Randal L. Kottwitz, Maralee Leach, Liz Lee, Jo Leyland, Terri Licking, Deb Loseke, Randy Lukasiewicz, Roselyn McFarland, Cindy Miesbach, Amber Mohr, Ruth Alice Maurice, Lee Meyers, Judi Meyer, Nebraska Department of Economic Development, Nebraska Division of Travel and Tourism, Karen Nelson, Lissa Nelson, Shirley Niemeyer, Jean Norman, Gary and Diane Ober, Scott Oliva, Alice Osterman, Gary Peterson, Sharon Priefert, Julie Powell, Bob Sautter, Betty Sayers, Deb Skinner, Bill Slovinski, Jim Smith, Cindy Stec, Charles Strinz, Sue Ann Switzer, Andela Taylor, Jessica Tschirren, Lee Warneke, Sue and Kent Worker, and Mary Zimmerman.

★ ★

Stretching from the high lonesome plains of eastern Colorado to the meagerly populated western caucuses of Iowa and pinched between the oppressive expanses of South Dakota and Kansas, Nebraska is well known to most Americans as " . . . one of those big square states in the middle, right?"

Residents of both coasts take pride in their ignorance of places like Nebraska and have long done so. One of the earliest maps of the area made during the American westward expansion was produced by Major Stephen H. Long's scientific expedition in 1821. On that map, the area now known as Nebraska was described as part of the Great American Desert, thereby seeding the national consciousness with the mental image of Nebraska as a place to "keep moving, folks, nothing to see here."

Turns out that with a little irrigation, crops like corn and soybeans and corn and wheat and corn grow here like gangbusters. America's Breadbasket, they called it in the mid-1900s, a straightforward and productive place focused on essential commodities, not the frivolous coastal concerns of style and power. Most travelers don't really experience Nebraska. They peer down at it from 30,000 feet as east-west flights plow the sky in parallel rows. For them, the quiltlike pattern of farm country represents a vast interruption. Nowadays they call it Fly-over Country.

Motorists similarly suffer the mind-numbing expanses along I-80 with an attitude described long ago by renowned Nebraska author Mari Sandoz:

"[Nebraska] usually is characterized as 'that long flat state that sets between me and anyplace I want to go.'"

Nebraska deserves better treatment. TV newscasters and Chamber of Commerce types now combat previous unflattering designations with a new descriptor, The Heartland, hoping to connect with the collective national memory of farms, fresh eggs, home-baked pies, hard work, and Auntie Em-ish faces opening perpetually unlocked doors. Truth is, that's a more accurate description, never mind Charlie Starkweather or

introduction

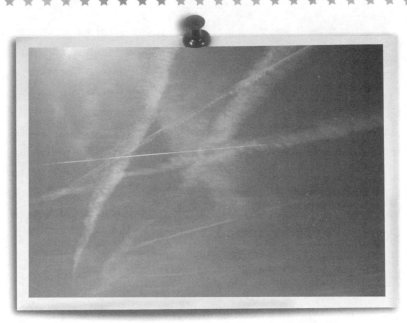

The trails across Nebraska once had names like Oregon, Pony Express, Mormon, Lewis and Clark, or Deadwood. Now the most prominent trails are these: contrails.

the longtime home to the central brain of the operations department of the military-industrial bombplex at Offutt Air Force Base.

At the same time, Nebraska deserves its stereotypes as much as any other state. It is mostly flat and practical-minded. That's why you can ask around at a dinner party in Los Angeles or New York and everyone who's been through the state will have the same unflattering reaction. It's roughly the same response as you'll get if you ask those same urbanites if they've ever had a colonoscopy. This book will not change the overwhelming national perception. But it will tell you about places you've never been, like Colon, Nebraska. More on that later.

So accept the invitation to celebrate the stereotypical as well as the antithetical. Enlightened residents can use it as a coping mechanism; visitors can embrace it as both a cultural and countercultural guide.

That Corn Is A-maize-ing

The educated reader knows of Nebraska's more notable contributions to America's character and rich history, of its populist politics, the lore of the Pony Express Trail, the start of the transcontinental railroad, and the origins of Arbor Day. But we can be candid here—you ain't too educated. When you think of Nebraska, your mind floods with images of football and the wholesome taste of corn on the cob.

A word on words: The grain Nebraskans call corn is known as maize in much of the world. Etymologically speaking, corn is a collective noun for grain and could refer to wheat as well. In fact, biblical scholars will point out that when Ruth worked in a field of corn, the grain was in fact wheat. In Nebraska, corn means corn.

Corn is a way of life here—and is seen among local economic development types as fueling the road to national energy salvation. Ethanol production has created a new economic engine in the local economy. It has been said that modern agriculture is the science of turning petroleum into food. Now it has become the science of turning petroleum into ethanol, a petroleum additive.

The future of ethanol is uncertain, but one thing is sure: The ever-inventive farmer (and the state's congressional delegation) will think of new, subsidized uses for Nebraska's bountiful crop. Perhaps a new rural industry will blend ethanol with another popular, locally produced chemical, methamphetamine. Imagine a fuel combining meth and ethanol—they could call it ethamphetamine, or eth for short. Now there's a fuel that could get visitors from one end of the state to the other in a really big hurry.

★ ★

Bottom line, there's plenty to see here. You just need to get off I-80 and slow down. Or you can speed through the state with this handy guide to tell you what you're missing. Either way, you will no longer think of Nebraska simply as one of those indistinguishable states in the nation's agricultural midriff. Instead you'll have fond memories of some of the quirks that characterize its surprising, if subtle, landscape and its modest but alert populace, folks who get the joke even if they don't always let you know it.

1

Northeast

*T*he great westward expansion into this part of Nebraska began in earnest for the very young United States of America with the Lewis & Clark Corps of Discovery in 1804. While the corps primarily stayed the path of the Missouri River valley, Private George Shannon, a corps member mentioned more than once in the journals

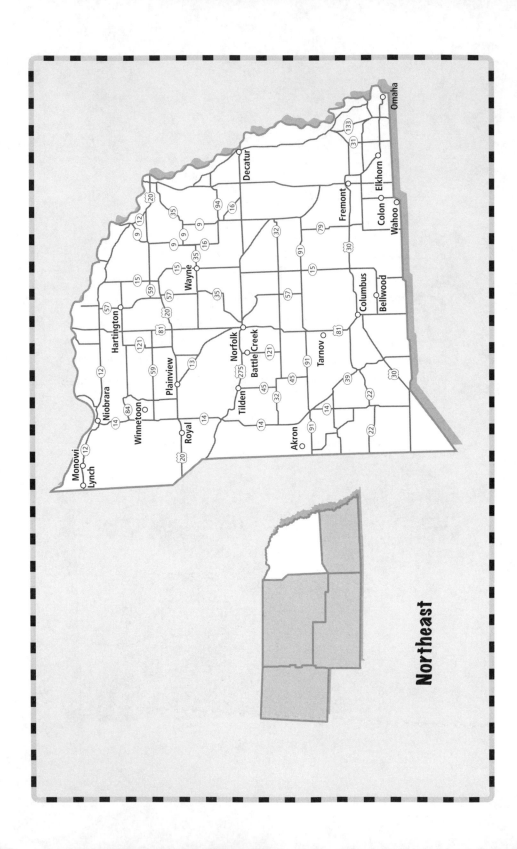

Northeast

for his meager orienteering skills, took an unintentional side trip while looking for lost horses. It was close to here that Private Shannon spent sixteen days trying to find his way back to the group, making do with some scavenged wild grapes and one rabbit. After retiring from exploring the wilds of western America, he took up law and put his keen orienteering skills to good use as a US senator representing Missouri.

This part of Nebraska looks most like neighboring Iowa and Minnesota, relatively well populated, with both people and trees dotting the rolling hills. The northern border of this part of the state is graced with an exceptionally picturesque river valley, which is slowly being discovered by well-heeled urbanites seeking their private and as-yet-undiscovered beautiful respite from overpopulated parts of America. For a while this part of the Great Flyover can still offer seclusion and a much less hectic pace of life. If instant messaging and Internet connections are important to your lifestyle, bring your own satellite dish. It's a good place to get lost.

It Takes a Child to Raise a Village
Akron

Mr. O'Brian lives about halfway between Albion and Spaulding, closest to the now nonexistent town of Akron. A farmer/rancher and enthusiast of days gone by, O'Brian spent many weekends over the years at farm sales, picking up the items that modernization and fashion made obsolete. His collection of sandstone grinding wheels, harrows, horseshoes, and other items he could put in or pull behind a pickup grew larger than can be found in most county museums. His collection includes tractors, steam engines, and many mechanical marvels that cost his farming peers an arm, leg, or fingers prior to the days of safety guards on moving equipment and warning labels on ladders.

The collection wouldn't be so unusual if O'Brian's penchant for collection was limited to the devices of agricultural production and family farm artifacts, except for the sheer numbers—not even Minden's famous Pioneer Village has the number of many items on display that O'Brian has in his collection. What sets this collection apart is the fact that O'Brian also bought buildings to create his own town; he has more buildings than some towns in Nebraska! A church, schoolhouse, train depot, home, and store are all visible from the road. One of his daughters tells the tale that she spent a summer when she was in high school working with her siblings and father to build a sod house. "Not my favorite summer," she said. "I would have had more fun playing golf."

Whatever the reason for the collection, after years of inviting his fellow enthusiasts and neighbors out to his place to fire up the sawmill and steam engines, he hasn't done so in years. So now, O'Brian's "town" is slowly becoming another ghost town of Nebraska—only one that was never actually populated.

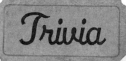

Nebraskans are children of the corn. The fictional town of Gatlin, Nebraska, is the backdrop of the Stephen King short story "Children of the Corn" that also made it to the silver screen along with several sequels.

As ye sow, so shall ye reap. Grim.
Dani Simmonds (corn) and Brooke Zaras (sign)

★ ★

Not Cowpie, Doll, It's Kewpie
Battle Creek

In the early 1900s, back when boys wore knickers and women wore Edwardian-era big hair, bigger hats, and long dresses with tiny waists, onetime Battle Creek resident Rose O'Neill was the highest-paid female illustrator in the country. An editor from the *Ladies Home Journal* collected several cupidlike images O'Neill used as background for

Pixies are perched on poles in Battle Creek.

★ ★

some romance stories and asked her to create a series of illustrations around them. O'Neill drew the cupidlike images and created verse about these carefree elfish characters she called Kewpies (pronounced QUE-pee), and the first version was published in December 1909. The immediately popular Kewpies took the country by storm.

O'Neill went on to write three Kewpie books, and her Kewpie Kutouts were the first double-sided paper dolls published for popular consumption. Either on a whim or with incredible marketing insight (remember that this was seventy years before the Star Wars toy boom, long before movie character toys were standard Happy Meal fare), she agreed to a line of dolls and figurines and eventually to lamps, dishes, postcards, fabric, china, glassware, wallpaper, picture frames, and jewelry. The Kewpie Doll became as big of a national phenomena as the Cabbage Patch dolls of the '80s or the Beanie Babies and Tickle Me Elmo dolls of the '90s.

Rose started her career when she won the *Omaha World Herald*'s contest for young illustrators. She did so well with her entry, in fact, that the fact-checking editors invited her to come in and demonstrate her ability prior to announcing the contest results. A copy of her winning entry, "Temptation Leading Down Into the Abyss," is in the Heritage Museum in Battle Creek's Park of Pride Arboretum. Battle Creek, the town where she spent the early part of her childhood, has lovingly kept the memory of her pioneering life there alive.

Who knows where the largest collection of Kewpie dolls in the country exists today? Perhaps those who attend the annual gathering of Kewpie aficionados called Kewpiestas can tell you. But in Battle Creek, Nebraska, local enthusiasts are working hard to grow the Kewpie collection you can find at the local insurance company. Where many towns have decorated their downtown light poles with banners, flags, or seasonal decorations, Battle Creek has cut and posted metal sculptures of the dolls in impish positions to let the visitor know of the local ties to the once-national craze. They could do worse—in the words of O'Neill, the Kewpies get into trouble, but they " . . . get themselves out, always searching out ways to make the world better and funnier."

The Mutual Insurance Heritage Museum is located at 603 South Preece Street in the Parks of Pride Arboretum. Call (402) 675-2925, (402) 675-8185, or (402) 675-5006 for access.

It's a Lumberjack, and It's Okay
Bellwood

On the north side of NE 64 about 5 miles west of Bellwood stands an oversize lumberjack above a well-manicured lawn. It's easily 25 feet tall, but with no sign or insignia to inform the curious traveler

This Jack looms more than lumbers.

of its intent or meaning, one can only muse about its significance. Is this some remembrance of an ancestor of local Scandinavian farmers, or homage to a tall tale of why the plains are treeless, or some nose-thumb directed to Mr. Bell, the tree planter for whom nearby Bellwood was named? Perhaps the songs of Monty Python are more inspirational than we thought.

You can see the giant lumberjack 5 miles west of Bellwood on the north side of NE 64 (2 miles east of the junction of NE 64 and US 81).

Mowin' in the Wind

Bellwood

If you think I-80 has a lot of traffic, you should have been around during the mass migration of the mid-1800s. Fortune hunters and religious refugees with more determination than good sense piled their families into covered wagons and followed well-worn trails westward along the Platte River. Despite 150 years of agriculture since then, remnants of those pioneer highways can still be found.

Gerald Mick is pretty sure the Oxbow Trail crossed his family's farmland 4 miles west of Bellwood, though any ruts have long since been plowed under. In 1997 he decided to salute those sturdy folks . . . in a big way. He built life-size replicas of a family and two ox-driven wagons and placed them in a park setting on a rise out behind his house. He planted native grasses, trees, and shrubs and excavated a pond to add to the parklike setting.

The Oxbow Pioneer Memorial Park is set well back from the road, and you've got to pay attention to notice the engraved wooden sign announcing it. The memorial ought to be to the man who built it and keeps the grass mowed, for it is his vision and work that created and maintains this stucco-rich interpretation of the hardworking independents who moved west along this trail. If you stop by this private-but-open-to-the-public park, you're likely to see Gerald puttering around in a golf cart and doing his best to add to this sanctuary for flora and fauna. He organized the park as a nonprofit corporation years

Westward ho! Gerald Mick is so sure the Oxbow Trail crossed his family's land that he built a life-size replica of some traveling pioneers.

ago, but he says, "I haven't raised a dime. I don't have that skill and I don't have the time." You can find the park 2 miles west of Bellwood on the south side of NE 64 (5 miles east of the junction of NE 64 and US 81).

Inflaming Colon

Colon

Nebraska has several towns with unique names, such as Bee, Surprise, Wahoo, and Winnetoon. Nebraska is the westernmost state in the United States with a town named Colon; the others are Georgia, Michigan, North Carolina, and Pennsylvania. One can't ruminate on the name of this town long before potential slogans come to mind:

Full of regular people.

We're on the move.

Scope us out!

Don't be an ass, stop in Colon.

Colossal!

A side trip, not an endpoint.

Make a full stop here.

All's well that ends well.

No ifs, ands, or butts about it.

Head on in.

Warm to the core.

It's always 96.61 degrees (longitude) in Colon.

Introducing: Colon!

You get out of it what you put in.

Gutsy.

Join the movement.

Take the plunge into the Colon swimming pool.

★ ★

Unfortunately, with a population of only 138, and set off the main highway, residents here haven't put up a sign, much less invested cold hard cash in a slogan.

At least one local knows a good opportunity for promotion when she sees it. The very first "Rollin' to Colon" bicycle tour in the nation took place in Nebraska in March 2006, organized by Holly Rochelle, a colon cancer survivor. This local fund-raising ride to promote colon cancer awareness began in Omaha and traveled a transverse 50 miles west before descending into Colon.

Another educational effort, the Colossal Colon, visited Omaha in 2005. Coco, as it is known to its caretakers, did not make a side trip to Colon. Too bad. A picture of a 4-foot-diameter, 40-foot-long plasticized colon surrounded by 100 or so residents of Colon is an image that would have any local editor saving paper for the story.

Crimping Iron
Columbus

One doesn't have to travel very far in Nebraska or around much of the agricultural parts of the world in order to find Behlen metal panel grain bins, sporting a silvery sheen of galvanized wavy metal. Walter Behlen, a founder of Behlen Manufacturing Company, wanted to demonstrate that his metal building materials could be used for just about anything. In 1958 Walter and his wife, Ruby, built their new home out of Behlen corrugated panels.

Fifty years later, the 7,100-square-foot house looks great from the outside, and because it is painted brown, it blends in so well with the neighborhood the casual passerby might not even notice it. The Behlen family donated the home to the Columbus Community Hospital Foundation, which in turn sold it to a nice local couple who are redoing the inside of the home.

Walter built this house three years after one of his corrugated steel buildings "survived" an atomic blast in the Nevada desert. That building, 1.25 miles from the detonation site of a 30-kiloton A-bomb,

Now that's what you call steel 'n home.

ended up with its roof dented, sides warped, windows gone, and wood door splintered, but it stood nonetheless. In the early 1960s these bomb test results provided advertising fodder for a line of Behlen Family and Community Fallout and Blast-Resistant Shelters, using former Nebraska governor Val Peterson as a pitchman.

Those Cold War family blast or fallout shelters weren't sold with the same conveniences of Walter's home. When purchased, the home had two large open rooms to be used for entertaining and two St. Charles kitchens with metal (of course) cabinetry. Some non-corrugated features included a cork floor, Burmese teakwood, and Mount Shuksan granite. The Behlens enjoyed entertaining, as demonstrated by the family's guest book, which holds signatures of visitors from around the world, including those signed in from Brazil, Japan, South Africa, and Palestine.

The Behlens' house is located at 2555 Pershing Road.

* *

1876 Was a Pretty Good Year

Glur's Tavern opened in 1876 and claims to be the oldest continuously operating tavern west of the Missouri River. That was the year that Rutherford B. Hayes beat Samuel Tilden for president, Alexander Bell invented the telephone, the *Harvard Lampoon* was founded, Mark Twain published *The Adventures of Tom Sawyer*, and Crazy Horse whupped George Armstrong Custer at Little Big Horn.

The tavern is located at 2301 Eleventh Street in Columbus; call (402) 564-8615 for more information.

Heads and Tales

Decatur

The dynamic and forceful Omaha Chief Blackbird is buried atop Blackbird Hill 8 miles north of Decatur on what was historically a "native American power point and vision quest ritual site" (according to Brad Olsen's *Sacred Places North America: 108 Destinations*). Petroglyphs in the rock base near the river attest to the importance of this spot. Four years after Chief Blackbird died of smallpox, Lewis and Clark described the burial spot in their August 11, 1804, journal entry as "a mound of earth about 12 feet diameter at the base, & 6 feet high is raised over him turfed . . . "

George Catlin, who was trained as a lawyer but famous as a contemporary painter of Native American life, told the tale that Chief Blackbird had been buried in full dress and fully equipped, upright and astride his warhorse along with his bow, medicine bag, tobacco pouch, and the scalps he had taken from his enemies. That tale was popular among new settlers, symbolizing either the special bond between a man and his steed or the emotions of those who would seek to honor the memory of Blackbird. But current members of the Omaha tribe tend to discount the story of Blackbird buried upright on his horse.

Catlin also claimed that while he was visiting this mound in 1832, he discovered the hole in the mound, and with a little work on that hole, he found the skull of the chief, which he took with him back to the Smithsonian.

Blackbird Hill is not open to the public, which may be just as well given the slightly more modern, and more timeless, story associated with it. This other tale is one of true love, rejected love, and death. The particulars vary depending on the telling, but the essence is as follows:

In the 1840s a young couple were deeply in love. Before they married, the young man left on a journey and did not return. After waiting for many years, the young woman married another and moved west with her husband to start a new life. Her true love did eventually return, and learning of her move west, he chose to follow after her. After some time he gave up his long search, but on his trip homeward he happened across his love near a cabin on Blackbird Hill. They were thrilled to find each other, and the woman asked him to wait as she broke the news to her husband. The husband stabbed his wife in a rage, then gathered her up, bleeding, and ran to the cliff at the top of Blackbird Hill. Without pausing, he leapt off the precipice, still clutching the woman, who screamed as they both plummeted to their deaths. Those who know the area say that the bloodstained ground between the former cabin and the spot where the couple went over the edge is still barren, 150 years after the incident.

It's said that every October 17, the anniversary of their deaths, you can hear the ghostly, ghastly screams echo up and down the Missouri

Crop Circles

We shouldn't be too tough on those early cartographers who labeled Nebraska as the heart of the Great American Desert. At the time, it was functionally true. In the early decades of territorial expansion, it was water, or the lack of it, that bedeviled homesteaders interested in growing crops. More than one entrepreneurial spirit used people's dust-driven desperation to turn a dollar on rainmaking devices. These contraptions operated concussively, either firing off boxes of dynamite with megaphone-like amplifiers pointed toward the skies or by releasing a flotilla of balloons or kites with explosive charges set to go off nearer to cloud level. These ear-shattering examples and others were funded in Nebraska by an organization known as the "Rain God Association."

In the 1880s the popular belief was that "rain follows the plow." As more prairie was turned into cropland, more rain would fall. But this wasn't really true until 1949, when Nebraska tinkerer Frank Zybach invented a device known as the center pivot, a sprinkler system that moistens large circles of farm crops, creating attractive patterns visible from 30,000 feet in the air.

The crop circles in Nebraska are mostly full of corn. So many movies (*Children of the Corn, Signs, The X Files, Field of Dreams*) have used a scene in a cornfield to develop fear and suspense that it's no wonder people of a coastal persuasion choose to fly over corn country—they're petrified at the thought of what lies hidden behind the roadside wall of corn.

Center pivots are now pumping water out of the ground faster than rainfall can replenish the ocean of fresh water under Nebraska. Before too long we may exhaust the water supply by growing corn to turn into ethanol to power our farm machinery . . . to grow corn.

From 30,000 feet, the prairies look as pixelated as a censored gesture on commercial TV. NASA/GSFC/METI/ERSDAC/JAROS and U.S./Japan ASTER Science Team

River valley near Blackbird Hill. You'll need to pull out your earbuds and pay close attention to judge for yourself whether these wraiths still wander the bluffs of the Missouri.

Blackbird Hill is located on the Omaha reservation but not open to the public. You can reach the Blackbird Scenic Overlook on the Omaha Reservation at milepost 152 on US 75, about 3 miles north of Decatur. For more information, call (402) 837-5301.

Going Mooclear
Elkhorn

The first cattle fallout shelter survival test began in Elkhorn eighteen years to the day after the bombing of Hiroshima on August 6, 1963, conducted by the Office of Civil Defense and the US Department of Agriculture. The *Nebraska Farmer* magazine reported on the two-week event by saying, "In the future, a number of farmers will be thinking about remodeling some existing structure or constructing a new dual-purpose building that will serve not only as a hog house or dairy barn but also as a fallout shelter." Publicity of the test was widespread, getting national television coverage on NBC and in news-papers in forty-seven states.

The Roberts Dairy Company, headquartered in nearby Omaha, sponsored the event and built a 108-foot by 45-foot (4,860 square feet) underground concrete structure designed to hold one hundred cows and two bulls. For the two-week-long event, the structure held thirty-five bred Guernsey cows, one bull, and two University of Nebraska–Lincoln animal husbandry seniors who tended to the cattle.

The students, Ike Anderson and Dennis DeFrain, ate canned goods, Nebraskits (see the Nuclear Age Cracker Barrel sidebar), and mixes of powdered drinks when they weren't feeding cattle, reading books, playing chess, or reporting on their activities in journals. While in radio contact from their bunker, they reported that they had gotten used to the smell after the first two days, but they "especially missed cold milk." Hearing this, the president of Roberts Dairy met these

★ ★

Interesting ag-fact: Cows produce about 15 percent of the world's atmospheric methane. Dennis DeFrain

underground herdsmen as they left the shelter on August 20 with a pitcher of cold milk and a supply of sweet rolls.

Asked if they would participate in another shelter test, one said politely, "Well, we don't want to look at another cow for a couple of weeks."

SPAM Factory
Fremont

Only two Hormel factories in the world make the delectable treat known as SPAM. One of these factories is in Austin, Minnesota, and the other is in Fremont. While the factory in Minnesota enjoys its exclusiveness by hosting a visitors' museum and putting up billboards miles away to attract visitors, the Fremont facility keeps a low profile. One cannot find a trace of the iconic blue and gold logo anywhere on the outside of the facility.

The only time the local factory seeks public attention is during the Fremont Days celebration, when a SPAM van rolls into town and experts judge the local SPAM recipe contest.

Other than that, only one clue is available to the SPAM detective looking for the factory: 50,000 hogs arrive daily at a building by the railroad tracks in the industrial part of town.

What happens then is anyone's guess.

Rawhide!
Fremont

Rawhide Creek flows west to east on the northern edges of Fremont. The gruesome story about how it got its name comes from many sources, none of which have come from any eyewitness to the

"Nuclear Age Cracker Barrel"

At a time when people were encouraged to prepare for nuclear attack, the State of Nebraska Department of Agriculture created "a family of Nuclear-Age Foods" called Nebraskits, which its enthusiastic marketing copy described as "palatable to all age groups." These Nebraska-shaped wafers were made of surplus grain and came in multiple delicious flavors—wheat, corn, milo, and milo-wheat—and were developed to "offer hope for the hungry, survival for the prepared."

★ ★

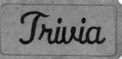

Trivia

The Omaha Public Power District (OPPD) owns and operates the smallest US commercial nuclear power plant. It has an electrical output of 470 megawatts.

supposed actual event. The story may be only folklore, some pre-urbanization urban legend told on the prairies to reinforce the rules of engagement of the day.

The details of the story vary depending on the source, but the framework is consistent among them all. A group of pioneers on their way to make their fortunes during the California Gold Rush had in their midst a young man who made no secret of the fact that he intended to shoot and kill the first Indian he saw. It was near here that he saw one and made good on his boast. When the poor dead fellow's friends heard the noise and learned of the deed, they stopped the travelers and demanded that the culprit be given to them. The travelers gave him up, not wanting to make the individual's crime their own. As the group watched in horror, the young man was tied to a tree and skinned alive. Thus, the creek was named Rawhide to remind others of plains justice.

Carving Knife
Hartington

There was a time in America when a father gave his son a pocketknife as a rite of passage. In that time, the penknife was more common to the pockets of boys and men than cell phones or car keys. If a young man turned out his pockets in the principal's office in those days, the penknife was as likely a find as a Bazooka Joe comic.

There's Land-locked, and There's Land-Incarcerated

A state is considered landlocked if it is not bordered on any side by a body of water (except rivers). The United States has many such states. Eleven states—Colorado, Illinois, Indiana, Iowa, Kansas, Missouri, Nebraska, South Dakota, Utah, Wisconsin, and Wyoming—qualify as doubly landlocked, which means they are surrounded by landlocked states.

But Nebraska is the only state that can claim to be trebly landlocked, which means all the states surrounding it (Colorado, Kansas, Missouri, Iowa, South Dakota, and Wyoming) are doubly landlocked. In this respect, Nebraska is clearly the center of the United States.

It's not that Nebraskans are thalassophobic (fearful of the sea). It's more that they are just a little bit anti-coastal.

The emphasis is on "land."

★ ★

The knives were used in a schoolyard game of chicken called mumblety-peg, but only after boys had learned to consistently throw their knife blade-first into the ground. With some consistency at that throw, the contest moved to pairs who would each try throwing their knife closest to the other's foot. A bad throw would cause the loser greater shame than the winner's physical injury. Today it would cause at least one expulsion and multiple lawsuits.

This chain is forged from a matchstick.

Prior to the infestation of television, the milestones for the young knife owner were gaining a good working knowledge of wood types, carving a willow whistle, and earning a spot on the porch next to the elder whittlers.

Many young men left the craft at two or three finely honed pointy sticks, useful for roasting hot dogs and marshmallows. But some who were born of these years, like Hugo Wuebben, became masters. The Cedar County Historical Museum has Wuebben's complete works, all done with a penknife like the ones so many born of his time had in their pockets, given them by their fathers. The collection includes plaques, gavels, and many miniatures. One of the smallest of the lot is the wooden match-length chain, whittled from (of course) a matchstick.

The chain is a little hard to find: You will need a chair to look up high on the wall in the display cases of his smallest works. See if you can find the working pliers that are only 1.5 inches long, too. While you are looking, consider the hours spent carving all of the art products you see, and the hours of sharpening you can't.

The Cedar County Historical Museum is located at 304 West Franklin Street.

Black, White, and Red All Over
Lynch

What's black and white and red all over? You won't find a zebra with a sunburn at the Weeder place north of Lynch (for that you might try Zoo Nebraska at Royal). You will find a delectable collection of Outsider Art, both in the yard in front of the house on the west side of the road, and amid the trees and lawns as you head north.

White. Red. Black. These are the colors one sees throughout Nebraska—something to do with a long-held autumn tradition of weekend gatherings honoring Nebraska's huskers of corn. But here, these are the colors of a spray paint palette for folk artistry, honoring the masters and personal visions alike.

★ ★

Several Nebraska fencerows have fitted upturned boots on top of the wooden posts—providing some kind of added protection against the weather, or a personal statement that these boots are no longer made for walkin'. At Weeder's, about 2 miles south of Old Baldy, the artist spray paints the posts white and the boots red. When the paint can is emptied, it's pinned to the top of a bootless post.

If you look at the fences around the house, miniature murals the size of automobile hoods (that's because they are automobile hoods) are lined up as panels of a fence, each with their own unique treatment. Mixed in with the spray-painted hoods are some figurines, and an occasional W made from hanging rope.

Neither rain, nor hail, nor exuberant art will keep the postman from his appointed rounds.

"Barking Squirrels"

Old Baldy, as the formation near Lynch is now known, was labeled "The Tower" by the Lewis and Clark expedition. There are nineteen other states that have at least one geographical feature with the name, but this is the only one where the crew of the Corps of Discovery formed a bucket brigade from the Missouri River and spent half a day pouring enough water into the burrowed homes of what we now call prairie dogs to flush one out. The captive "barking squirrel" survived the rigors of the trip and was presented, alive, to President Thomas Jefferson.

Even here, in rural, remote Nebraska, where the nearest neighbor isn't even in view, the old axiom still holds true: "Good fences make good neighbors."

To find Weeder's, take Fourth Street north out of Lynch about 5 miles, and look to the west side of the road.

Rudy's Library
Monowi

For people of a certain age and fans of Iowan Meredith Wilson, the stereotype of a small-town librarian is embodied by fictional Marian Paroo, the River City librarian in *The Music Man.* Never mind that the bespectacled shusher image bears no more resemblance to the knowledge managers and information architects of our digital age than does the image of a husking peg on the wrist of a champion corn shucker to a $400,000 combine. Stereotypes change much slower than does reality.

Librarians are defenders of our public goods, battling free-riders who want the benefits of information access without paying a share

★ ★

of the cost, and providing frontline defense against the greed of intellectual property rights advocates who, if their thinking held sway in the time of Benjamin Franklin, would never have allowed our current lending library to see the light of day. Libraries are often forced to survive on the crumbs of the public budget left over by other public programs.

So when Monowi (population 1), a town without a fire department, gas station, church, school, town hall, or fire hydrant, opened its own library, librarians around the country took notice.

It started with Rudy Eiler's vision and hard work. Rudy, Elsie's dear departed husband, built the library near the tavern that Elsie still operates. His dream was to move his collection of books to the building, but the job took longer than Rudy had left on this earth. When he

Plan to attend the *Nebraska Curiosities* book signing at the library.

passed, the population of Monowi halved, and the dream was left to Elsie.

Elsie, in her quiet, no-nonsense way, made it happen. And then the world took notice. The library was written up by the *Omaha World Herald*, the *Los Angeles Times*, *The Observer* in London, and the *Times* in New York, and the story was republished by other papers throughout the world. Television networks followed, plus mentions in more books than the one in your hand.

Monowi has long promoted its position as the smallest town in the state, starting way back when it had six residents. That laid-back promotion through sales of caps and koozies that proclaim Monowi as "Nebraska's Smallest" is housed in the roadside Monowi Tavern. Rudy's Library and Elsie's élan earned greater notoriety for Monowi than those sales, reaching a larger audience through worldwide press and Internet coverage than perhaps even that of Omaha, which spends at least $1 for each of its 427,872 citizens.

Just another example that Bob Dylan was right: "The order is rapidly fadin'."

The library is located just to the north of the tavern on the northeast corner of Broad Street and NE 12. To get the key and peruse the collection, stop in the tavern at 9 Broad Street and talk to Elsie. For more information, call (402) 569-3600.

Bigfoot Ranch
Niobrara

Amateur cryptozoologist, writer, rancher, and adventurer Danny Liska grew up working several hundred acres of land between Verdigris and Niobrara. The land, on the east side of NE 14, overlooks the Niobrara River and offers the attuned visitor a peek back to a time before paved highways were bordered by stick-built homes.

If there is any place in this part of America's Flyover where the infamous Bigfoot might roam, where snakes grow as big around as a gallon jug, where UFOs regularly visit, or where halflings keep watch

If you look closely, you can see Bigfoot under the palm tree.

as Danny Liska claimed in his books, this part of Nebraska offers a believable spot.

Danny interviewed and recorded in his books the tales told to him by his neighbors. Some of these stories were simply the newest incarnations of tales told by the people of the first nations on this continent. For example, the stories of the Little People, the Canotila, a people of 18 to 20 inches in height, were referenced by Lewis and Clark on August 24, 1804:

" . . . in this quarter is Suppose to be the residence of Deavels. that they are in human form with remarkable large heads, and about 18 Inches high, that they are very watchfull and are arm'd with Sharp arrows with which they Can Kill at a great distance . . . "

While the hill described in the journals of Lewis and Clark is on the South Dakota side of the Missouri River, Danny recorded sightings in several books to support his contention that the Little People indeed live nearby, along with the other strange fauna mentioned above. He was impressed with local tales of cryptozoology (the study of rumored or mythological animals for which conclusive proof does not yet exist), but it was the adventures he described in his first book that made him a cult legend.

That first book, *Two Wheels to Adventure*, self-published by Bigfoot Press in 1989, chronicles the road trip Danny began on his BMW motorcycle in 1959. He traveled from the northernmost point of road in America at the time, Circle City, Alaska, to the southern reaches of South America, finishing in 1962. The BMW people were so impressed with the feat that they gave him a new motorcycle, with which he went from the upper part of Norway down to South Africa during 1963 and 1964.

Danny's pioneering motorcycle trips provide inspiration to bikers today, as local bed-and-breakfast hosts can attest. Many bikers on their way up to Sturgis make a point to swing through the area to pay homage to one of motorcycling's first long-distance adventurers.

Or maybe they stop just to catch a glimpse of the Little People and other cryptids.

Trivia

"A lot of good people came out of Nebraska, and the better they were, the faster they came."

—Exchange between Johnny Carson and Dick Cavett, two famous former Nebraskans, as taken from *History of Nebraska* by James C. Olson and Ronald C. Naugle

★ ★

They're Grrreat

Another famous native son was Thurl Ravenscroft of Norfolk, voice of Kellogg's Frosted Flakes character Tony the Tiger for over fifty years and in over 500 television commercials. He also sang "You're A Mean One, Mr. Grinch" for the television edition of *How the Grinch Stole Christmas*.

Favorite Son
Norfolk

For thirty years Johnny Carson was the king of late-night comedy television. He started his entertainment career as The Great Carsoni in his hometown of Norfolk.

During his reign, he became the highest-paid and most-watched television personality. Carson's capacity for quips and comebacks is legendary, and some are still debated to this day.

One such debate, in which many still swear to have watched the show, revolves around an exchange between Johnny and legendary golfer Arnold Palmer (or his wife, in another variation). Johnny supposedly asks if Palmer and his wife have any pregame good luck rituals. The reply? Mrs. Palmer "kisses my balls." Johnny, using his quick wit, purportedly ad-libs, "That must make your putter stand up."

Whether you watched the show, or have done your own research into urban legends and doubt it ever happened, all can agree that the exchange is certainly in character for this star from the Heartland.

You won't find the answers to any controversies in Norfolk, but you can buy a tie. Carson generously selected items to be included in the Johnny Carson Gallery at the Elkhorn Valley Museum, which is located at 515 Queen City Boulevard. For more information, call (402) 371-3886.

★ ★

It Was a Clown
Plainview

Many children shy away from the first costumed merrymakers they meet. If it weren't for a quick association with sweets and swag, imagine how many early childhood encounters with Santa would turn into years of therapy—indeed, if therapists were to invent a social convention to be introduced to children as a way to create adult clients, could they make up anything more devious? Stephen King demonstrated his understanding of coulrophobia, a fear of clowns, when he created Pennywise, the antagonist in his 1986 book and 1990 ABC miniseries *It*. And Bart Simpson's insomniac catchphrase "Can't sleep, clown will eat me" (originally aired in 1992) provides a popular culture reference for both insomniacs and coulrophobics alike.

I ain't afraid of no clowns.

★ ★

The Klown Doll Museum in Plainview does not explore the dark side of clowns. If it did, the museum could likely raise funds by helping clown-fearing customers overcome their fears by facing them. Facing them? More like immersion therapy. Many museums offer groups an opportunity to overnight on the premises; while sleeping space is limited at the Klown Museum, imagine the opportunity of facing a fear of clowns by bedding down with its current displayed collection of over 2,000 clown dolls—over 4,000 clown eyes packed into close quarter, just watching, watching, watching . . .

The current collection makes this museum the largest collection of its kind in the United States, and the doll donations keep the museum staff scrambling for space. They have already expanded once and have enough clowns recently donated to expand again.

The museum collection is an extension of a longtime Plainview tradition of celebrating clowns, the Klown Festival, which has as part of its musical entertainment the Plainview Klown Band, playing oom-pah-pah entertainment in clown costumes.

While in the Klown Kapital of the United States, be sure to swing by the Foy George Memorial Band Shell in the park. See if the visit inspires you to conceive of another opportunity to celebrate with an emphasis on costumes and music.

The Klown Festival is held the first Saturday in June. The museum is open year-round and is located right on US 20 about midway through Plainview, just at the west end of Chilvers Park, south side of the road, southeast corner of Maple Street and Park Avenue.

For more information, call (402) 582-4433 or go to www.plvwtelco .net/clowndollmuseum.

TSI: Time Scene Investigation
Royal

Twelve million years ago in what is today Idaho, a volcano erupted more violently than Mount St. Helens, shooting one hundred times the amount of ash that St. Helens did into the atmosphere. Most

Check out the ash end of this critter.

schoolchildren have seen footage of the Mount St. Helens eruptions or have seen news coverage of billowing thick black clouds of smoke from vast forest fires. Modern-day travelers in the volcano-active "Pacific Rim of Fire" have seen light dustings from distant volcanoes, or perhaps have been waylaid because the fine material is abrasive to jet engines, therefore grounding outbound flights and detouring inbound flights. But these events pale when compared to the maelstrom of the midlands twelve million years ago.

The volcanic ash carpeted both heaven and the savannah in Nebraska. Around the watering hole, prehistoric rhinos, horses, turtles, camels, deer, and birds all drank as inches of ash fell and swirled around them. The inevitable, gasping mass fatality happened over several days. Some of the small and infirm died relatively soon, providing a feast of an easy last meal for carnivores, which lasted slightly longer. Through it all, the ash fell, providing a time line of death and

Whither the Weather?

"There's no such thing as bad weather, just bad clothes." That's an old Norwegian proverb, often used just before the phrase, "Now go outside and play."

Every state lays claim to weather woes, and in fairness to the other states of Flyover Country, Nebraska's is little better or worse. Gulf and Atlantic Coast residents confront the occasional broad devastation of hurricanes, but with enough lead time to panel over the windows or evacuate altogether; their weather creates little empathy here.

Authors/Dan Griggs Images

West Coasters suffer the threat of earthquakes (Nebraska has geologic faults, but they don't rock the boat), yet Californians who visit Nebraska seem terrified at the prospect of tornados. And why not? The unpredictable, random fury of a tornado can destroy a single home with pinpoint accuracy or wreak the vengeance of God on an entire town, leaving a spiraled, splintered sprawl in its wake. Careful study of tornados in Nebraska tells us they can strike at any time of day or night, any day of the year, but if previous performance is an indicator of future storms, then the risk is lowest in Nebraska in February, around 8:00 a.m.

A small tourism industry has developed around viewing and chasing tornados. People spend thousands of dollars to visit Nebraska or other spots along "Tornado Alley" for the privilege of possibly glimpsing this wanton destruction. Nebraska's tornado viewing is made more attractive by the near absence of hills to block the view of distant storms.

Nebraska offers a cornucopia of environmental phenomena, including thundersnow, floods, droughts, blizzards, dust storms, ice, fire, grasshoppers, hail, and locusts, to name a few. Some have been positively biblical in scope, others simply outside the norm for non-Nebraskans. It's not surprising for temperature swings to exceed 40, 50, or even 60 degrees in the span of a day. In fact, daily swings this far inland are about 50 percent larger than on the coasts.

Now you know the real reason for Nebraskans' legendarily poor fashion sense—their clothes are designed instead for common sense.

★ ★

dying for study today by paleontological investigators working on the site, discovered in 1971.

The Ashfall site offers an uncommon time capsule, an area of high preservation known as a lagerstatten in the archaeological field. No other high-quality, high-density collection of skeletal remains like this one has been found in the world. Due to a happy mix of water and minerals, these skeletons are preserved three-dimensionally just as they died, creating precious indisputable evidence of how the animals lived.

These animals are not the size of thunder lizards, but similar in size to animals on the prairies today. Visitors should appreciate the uniqueness of the preservation and an occasional surprise of animal type (such as the saber-toothed deer).

In 2006 the Department of the Interior named Ashfall the first National Natural Landmark in nearly twenty years. The park represents a cooperative effort of the University of Nebraska State Museum and the Nebraska Game and Parks Commission, which has intelligently designed a roof (known as the Rhino Barn) over a small portion of the dig and has plans for eventually constructing a much larger shelter over a larger part of the dig.

The Ashfall Fossil Beds State Historical Park is located at 86930 517th Avenue. For more information, call (402) 893-2000 or go to http://ashfall.unl.edu.

Nighttime is a Blast

Tarnov

A November 2004 Nebraska Travel and Tourism report cited an untapped tourism opportunity for Tarnov. It suggested that the area might "develop a new community festival based on the bombing of Tarnov."

In August 1943, during a WWII nighttime training mission gone awry, the bombardier mistook the town lights of Tarnov for an (arguably) nearby lighted bombing range. The bombs, which were practice casings weighted with sand, not explosives, were loosed and crashed into town well before dawn, waking residents, many of whom had been up into the wee hours that night enjoying an annual festival. Those who woke to the noise rousted neighbors to check for damage and injuries. Reports of a nearby barn fire further provoked the worries of townsfolk. When the sun rose and all were accounted for, Tarnov could laugh a little and catch up on lost sleep.

Townsfolk keep the memory of the bombing via some artifacts at the St. Michael Complex, but they are now considering a festival with a recognition of this historic event as a centerpiece. Hmmmm. What catchphrase would you suggest? The obvious phrase will not be mentioned here, so as not to perpetuate the tired stereotype of writers as often overly fond of drink.

Bombs away!

Tilden-itis
Tilden

While Kansas school boards continue to argue about the science or religion of human origins, the small Nebraska town of Tilden deals with the human origins of a religion called Scientology. Tilden is the birthplace of L. Ron Hubbard, the founder of Scientology. Hubbard, the man who famously said, "The best way to become a millionaire is to start a religion," is the founder of the Church of Scientology, which counts among its followers rich Hollywood movie stars and celebrities like Tom Cruise, Beck, Lisa Marie Presley, John Travolta, and Kirstie Alley. Many in the church think it would be a good idea to give the town money to memorialize Hubbard.

While other remote or rural small towns in Nebraska and nearby Iowa have swollen with pride and capitalized on their long-since-gone native sons or daughters—Donna Reed, Glenn Miller, Harold Lloyd, Johnny Carson—Tilden has gone out of its way to ignore its most famous expatriate.

In 1999 officials from the Church of Scientology learned that Tilden was struggling to come up with funds to upgrade its local park,

Two elders block the path of a leader of the flock.

so they offered more than $300,000 to help. Tilden's town fathers turned 'em down. Locals didn't like the idea of including something called "The Way to Happiness" trail with twenty-one stations along the path extolling the twenty-one Scientology precepts, things like "Take care of yourself. Do not murder. Do not steal. Honor your parents." During ensuing discussions, townsfolk also rejected a scaled-back suggestion naming a park shelter after Hubbard.

Instead, Tildenites have named a town park's ballfield after Richie Ashburn, the famed baseball player who was inducted into the Baseball Hall of Fame in 1995. In spite of plenty of literary evidence to the contrary, the fanaticism associated with the religion of baseball is less troubling—or perhaps it is because Ashburn represents a greater god.

We suggest that visitors swing through town playing recordings of poems and tunes penned by the local boy made good and sung by famous Scientologists like John Travolta. Be sure to tell the locals you are on your way to the Sandy Dennis Festival in Hastings.

★ ★

Wahoo!
Wahoo

Absurdist Late Show entertainer David Letterman moved the show's home office to Wahoo in March 1996. That was the last move for the home office. Wahoo is no longer credited as the source of the nightly Top Ten List; nor is any other town. The CBS Late Show Web page pays its respect to the last mentioned location with its show recaps section, entitled the Wahoo Gazette.

Wahoo lobbied hard to woo the home office away from Grand Rapids, Michigan, a much bigger community that served as the home

"Hello? Hello? Dave, is that you?"

★ ★

office for a year prior to the relocation. The change was announced after a graft contest, in which both communities tried their best to bribe the office location decision makers.

Wahoo offered, through the collaboration of the Nebraska governor, the honorary title of the Great Navy of the State of Nebraska and, with the help of others, several souvenir and gift items of under $100. Letterman jokingly pushed the graft contestants a little harder, and Wahoo sent a 1976 Ford Pinto with a sofa attached and a clock made of cow droppings.

When Larry King asked him to explain the home office choice in a 2002 interview, Letterman asserted that many people react to the world around them with a "wah."

"I'm the kind of guy that says wahoo—wahoo."

So consider: Do you wahoo?

Cluck Off!
Wayne

Twenty-five years of good cluck is represented by the repeat appearance of the Chickendale Dancers at the annual Wayne Chicken Show, which starts the second Friday in July. What began as a lark has become a proud male tradition, a yearly ritual, and a sacrament passed from friend to friend, father to son.

The Chickendales were not part of the first Chicken Show. The show began as a craft show and vendor fair and then gained

Trivia

"There are no Sundays west of Omaha."

—Character Charles "Slim" Honeycutt in the movie *The Cowboys*

What's the definition of "macho" man?

momentum by adding a parade and contests of skill and daring. But the Chickendales joined the parade early and have become mainstays.

The 'Dales began with the Commodore of the Wayne Yacht Club. His original concept began with a name, Chickendales, and a vision— a reality manhood version of the highly sculpted, fantasy-fleshed Chippendale dancers. The Commodore had many friends who looked the part of a "real man" (what part of this country doesn't have that in plentiful supply?), but they all balked at the thought they would be easily recognized by other Wayne-ians and would suffer unwanted comments on their (extra-?) ordinary shape.

So the creative Commodore, inspired by memory of the Unknown Comic and loaded with round-nosed scissors skills in the paper sack mask-making craft, created a costume design accessory that both eased the uneasiness of his Chickendale recruits and enhanced the chicken-ness of the outfits. And in the true spirit of camaraderie, none of the 'Dales reveals the identities of any who participate—it is a secret society of public dancers.

And every year the Chickendales' flatbed is in the parade, blaring an endless loop of the Village People performing "Macho Man" while it rolls down Main Street full of shirtless, farmer-tanned "real men" in paper sack masks, sunglasses, and shorts, who swivel their well-insulated six-pack abs for the parade crowd. The crowd cheers and women swoon as they pass by. Should any roadside viewer get swept up in the excitement and rush out to touch the 'Dales, the merciless squirt-gun-toting bodyguards swing into action on the ground, swarming the parade watcher and dousing her enthusiasm.

In 1998 the Chickendales received more coverage in the *National Geographic* article about Nebraska than did the omnipresent University of Nebraska Cornhusker football team. And the 'Dales point with pride to the fact that they are part of the US Folk Festivals section in the Smithsonian in DC. But the officials of Macy's Thanksgiving Day Parade turned them down, cold.

In each of the twenty-five years that the 'Dales have danced in the parade, a story has emerged, the mythology has grown. But the people have changed. Fathers handed off to sons, and the Commodore moved to Seattle, where word has it that he has done pretty well in the SPAM sculpting arena.

The Chickendales aren't the only reason to visit the Wayne Chicken Show. Both the cluck-off competition and the world's largest chicken dance are worth crowing about. But in this day of hyper hype of celebrities who are notable only for being noticed, the Chickendales represent a refreshing celebration of reality.

The Wayne Chicken Parade takes place on the second Saturday in July, during the Wayne Chicken Show, on Main Street. For more information go to www.myspace.com/chickendaledancers or www.chickenshow.com.

Privy Path
Winnetoon

When you're as far off the beaten path as Winnetoon, you need more than a unique name to attract visitors (the town bills itself as "the world's only Winnetoon"). So how about a collection of vintage outhouses? Gayle Neuhaus has gathered several and placed them discreetly behind a row of old buildings she assembled along the historic "Main Street" she created.

Teacher prepares for the day's lessons.

There's an old post office, a general store, a blacksmith shop, a school, and other historic buildings she saved from destruction. Neuhaus has a shop and office in the old post office, which conveniently serves as the town's active post office. She is happy to give tours (be sure to leave a donation, since it's the only support she gets for her heroic efforts), and her encyclopedic knowledge of area history makes the walk down Main Street Winnetoon even more authentic.

Don't miss the playful wood carvings scattered throughout the site. These were created by the late Cowboy Joe Serres, Neuhaus' partner, who managed the moving and reconstruction of this marvelous collection from bygone times. Neuhaus still describes the overall collection of artwork and history as "my dream and his nightmare." It's a refreshing example of fun and hard work that meets the eye of the traveler dedicated enough to travel to a town small enough that the post office looks quite a bit like the one in the General Store in Hooterville.

Main Street Winnetoon is a wonderfully authentic stab at turn-of-the-twentieth-century ambience, and it gives Winnetoon something it otherwise wouldn't have . . . a main street.

2

Lincoln and Omaha

*J*ust as most of the surface water in Nebraska drains eastward to the Missouri River, most of the population seems to have tumbled downhill and piled up at the eastern edge of the state in Omaha and, to a lesser extent, Lincoln. With almost half of Nebraska's population and nearly all of its traffic jams, Omaha is no longer the "twenty-minute city" it used to fancy itself. But that's okay, because "twenty-minute city" really means "there's nowhere to go here."

Omaha increasingly has many places to go. The city's downtown has staged an impressive renaissance, featuring the tallest building between Chicago and Denver, a performing arts center, an arena, and more condos than they'll ever be able to unload. And since the last renaissance here occurred around 1880, Omahans are more than ready to rock and roll. They've even fashioned a modest indie music scene.

At the heart of the new Omaha is the Missouri River. Omaha's riverbank used to be the back door to junkyards and lead refineries. Bums built shelters in the underbrush and gazed across to the Iowa side, where Iowa bums stared back. Then everything changed. It's as though somebody went for a walk one day and discovered a bona fide natural feature in a state noticeably short on mountains and coastlines. Since then, they've kicked out the homeless, built a pedestrian bridge across the Missouri, and stacked condos along its edge. What's next for Omaha: sailing lessons?

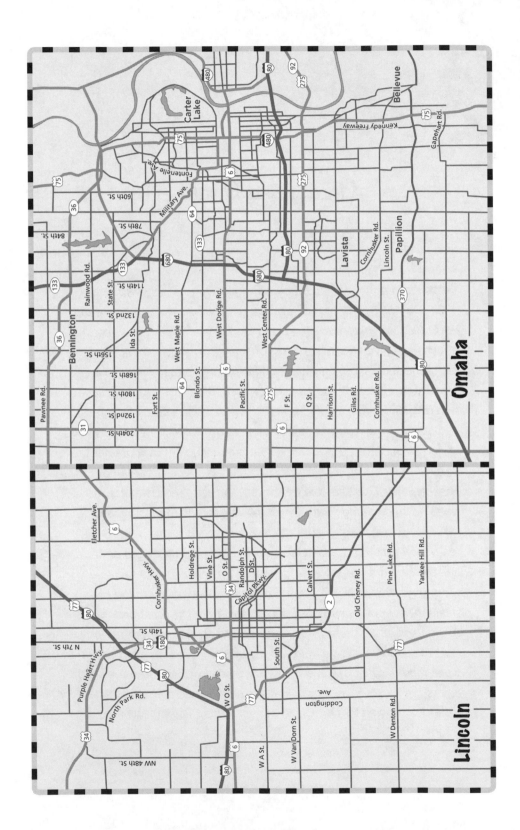

Lincoln and Omaha

★ ★

About one quarter of Nebraska's population of 1.7 million lives in Omaha proper, but the improper Omaha formed by the statistical legerdemain of economic development types emphasizes that Omaha is part of a 800,000 to 1.2 million population, depending on whether one counts only the nearby counties or all towns within a 50- to 60-mile radius. Unfortunately for many Nebraskans, that means they need to acknowledge the participation of proximate Iowans, and in doing that, they would need to give up half of the operating joke bank given them at birth:

Q: "What does IOWA stand for?" A: "Idiots Out Wandering About."

Q: "What is the best thing to come out of Iowa?" A: "I-80."

Or "Did you hear about the expansion at the Henry Doorly Zoo? They put a fence around Council Bluffs."

This area of Nebraska is gaining population while almost all of the rest of the state is losing. The areas that see the largest growth are on the farm-side edges of the town, as suburb-living children of farmers seek to move into areas with a view of open fields, views which in time are bartered away to developers of the next subdivision by farmers willing to cash in on the incredible increases in land value, who then either retire or move away from the encroaching cities to farm again.

Just west of Omaha lies the other major metropolitan center of the state, the capital city of Lincoln. Within the city boundaries sits the University of Nebraska Memorial Stadium, often and accurately described as the third largest Nebraska city on football game days. Lincoln wrested the capital away from Omaha when Nebraska became a state, and the two towns have nurtured a mythology of distinctions between themselves in an ongoing feud of one-upmanship. Which town is the better place to call oneself a Nebraskan? The question recalls the variously attributed observation about academic politics as "the most vicious and bitter form of politics, because the stakes are so low." With I-80 gaining more lanes between the two, and with both towns racing to annex land between them, it won't be long before such distinctions are largely academic.

★ ★

Mammoth Interest
Lincoln

Nebraska may be all about corn and football and corn in these modern, enlightened times, but if you climb in your Way Back Machine and dial up Nebraska twelve million years ago, you'd be surrounded by woolly mammoths, rhinos, giraffes, and camels (all wearing red football helmets!).

Some of them are on display at Morrill Hall, home to the University of Nebraska State Museum of Natural History on the UNL campus. Its exhibits are straight out of the 1950s, which makes them antiquated

An original copy of a dwarf mammoth.

Bug-Eatin' Grin

Back when territorial nicknames morphed into state names, when residents in Missouri were Pukes and those in Illinois were Suckers, Nebraskans were **Bug Eaters.** The name was likely related to biblically proportioned grasshopper invasions that stripped bare all plant life and much that wasn't nailed down besides. Reports of infestations so thick that residents were left with nothing to eat save bugs were probably the source of the name. Whatever the source, the name stuck and was one of the earliest team names for University of Nebraska football.

Football, as much as any sport, is built on tradition, and Nebraskans have long valued football as a national identity. It wasn't always so. A statewide Anti-Football Bill was actually proposed in the legislature by J.N. Gaffin back in the days of the Bug Eaters. It was prompted by the death of a football player at a game between Hastings and Doane Colleges.

How might the Husker Nation look today if Gaffin had been more persuasive?

in more ways than one. The hall is easy to find, thanks to the recent addition of a 5,000-pound bronze statue of Archie the Mammoth outside the main entrance.

Archie's bones are on display in Elephant Hall, touted by curators as one of the world's best displays of the evolution of elephants. The mammoth is the official Nebraska State Fossil, selected in part because of its plentitude—mammoth fossils have been found in all ninety-three Nebraska counties. In 1922 Lincoln County produced Archie, the largest of these finds; at a shoulder height of 14 feet, it is supposedly the largest articulated fossil mammoth skeleton on display in the world.

But it's neither the large skeleton nor the dated dioramas that makes this a worthy inclusion in this book. It is the contrasting display of a dwarf mammoth just in front of the world's largest mammoth skeleton. Dwarf mammoths evolved on islands near California, up in the Arctic, and in the Mediterranean, according to an evolutionary biology principle known as Foster's Rule.

The "dwarf mammoth" deserves an honored place right behind "jumbo shrimp" on the short list of oxymoronic animals.

The University of Nebraska State Museum of Natural History is on the main floor of Morrill Hall, which is located south of the intersection of Fourteenth and Vine Streets. It's open Monday through Saturday from 9:30 a.m. to 4:30 p.m. and Sundays and holidays from 1:30 to 4:30 p.m. It's closed New Year's Day, Thanksgiving, Christmas Eve, and Christmas Day. Admission is $5 for adults, $3 for children, and $10 for families. For more information, call (402) 472-2642 or go to www.museum.unl.edu.

Heartland Security Blanket

Lincoln

Did you know there are people who have built their academic careers and their jobs around the study of quilts? Such studies are a long way from the historic quilting bee gatherings and gabfests that entertained early Nebraska residents. Many in today's electronic entertainment-focused world don't understand quilt studies, but the University of Nebraska does. The university housed a quilt studies center in a broom closet for a decade until they could piece together enough private donations to fund the new $12 million International Quilt Studies Center and Museum.

This impressive facility opened in the spring of 2008, and it does justice to the largest publicly held collection in the world. Samples of the museum's 2,300-odd secured blankets are professionally displayed and

★ ★

described in their larger artistic context. The collection includes a faded white quilt from eighteenth-century France and a blood-spattered Civil War covering. The collection has fewer than one hundred "crazy quilts," the textile equivalent of a Jackson Pollack painting.

The new center gives scholars and tourists an unprecedented opportunity to expand their knowledge of quilting arts and history. The University of Nebraska does not yet have plans to establish a Department of Quilts, Bedsheets, and Miscellaneous Linens; however, we suspect that another $12 million donation might do the trick.

Don't be a wet blanket; when you are in Lincoln, be sure to visit.

The International Quilt Studies Center and Museum is located on the University of Nebraska–Lincoln East Campus, 1523 North Thirty-third Street. It's open Tuesday through Saturday from 10:00 a.m. to 4:30 p.m. and Sunday from 1:00 to 4:30 p.m. It's closed Monday, major holidays, and during university shutdowns. Admission is $5 for adults, $3 for students with school IDs and children (five to eighteen), $10 for families, and free for children four and younger. For more information, call (402) 472-6549.

Springweather and Starksteen

A string of murders by a former Lincoln trash collector, Charlie Starkweather, inspired Bruce Springsteen's song "Nebraska."

A perspective of Starkweather told locally is that when he and his underage girlfriend and fellow assassin Caril Ann Fugate were in custody and being moved from courthouse to jail, a reporter caught his attention and asked, "Why'd you do it?"

Charlie answered, "We were only trying to get out of town."

★ ★

When Thirty-six Is a Perfect Number

Lincoln

Thirty-six is the atomic number of krypton.

Thirty-six inches make up 1 yard.

Thirty-six is the sum of the cube of the first three numbers (13 + 23 + 33) and is also the sum of 1+2+3+4+5+6+7+8.

And thirty-six is the number of consecutive strikes one must make to get a perfect series in bowling.

In most sports, a "perfect game" is a matter of opinion. In bowling, all you have to do is knock down all ten pins twelve times in a row to record a perfect game score of 300. Statistically speaking, bowling's perfect game happens less often than does a no-hitter in professional baseball. It ain't easy, and yet tens of thousands of perfect games are celebrated every year.

This house belongs to Mr. 900.

Odd Museum

The Museum of the Odd in Lincoln is noted by various sources as one of the places that by every right should be in this book.

Everything about this "museum" is odd. Located in a sagging house tucked into a dicey neighborhood near acres of railroad tracks and no through streets for blocks, the only proof of its existence is an aged, unlit sign in the window. If it's winter, there won't be any footprints in the snow leading to the house—apparently the postal service doesn't even visit. No one answers the door. There is no phone number. Web site? You've got to be kidding. Odd indeed. The Odd Museum is located at 701 Y Street.

Bowling's truly elusive mark of perfection is the 900 series—three perfect games in a row. It had never been done in a sanctioned event until February 2, 1997, when a University of Nebraska sophomore named Jeremy Sonnenfeld hoisted his sixteen-pound Columbia Pearlized Pulse bowling ball and rolled thirty-six strikes in a row. It was a landmark in the history of a game that's been around for more than 1,500 years. One week later, for his success breaking the previous record of 899 (held by three bowlers), Sonnenfeld, now Mr. 900, was presented the first 900 series award by the American Bowling Congress.

It happened at Sun Valley Lanes in Lincoln, where—inexplicably—there is no shrine commemorating the event. Not even a laminated copy of the *New York Times* article about Sonnenfeld's achievement. Apparently bowlers, much like runners, don't look back.

If you go when leagues aren't playing, you can bowl the same six lanes where Sonnenfeld bowled during the tournament.

Sun Valley Lanes is located at 321 Victory Lane. For more information, call (402) 475-3469.

★ ★

Homage to the Original "Guide for Dummies"
Lincoln

Soon after its founding on the western edge of the expanding Modern American civilization, 120 years ago, the University of Nebraska at Lincoln was a premier institution, a recognized peer with Harvard. While it has not retained that high status among students of higher education, its host city of Lincoln contributed a product once known to almost all students—the CliffsNotes study guides. CliffsNotes, founded by Lincolnite Clifton K. Hillegass and known to all college graduates alive today who matriculated prior to the widespread use of the Internet, were the original black-and-yellow digest of all classic literature, from Homer's *Odyssey* to Steinbeck's *Grapes of Wrath*. The cover of CliffsNotes' guide to the Bible even graced the cover of *Time Magazine* in April 2007. These small pamphlets offered the student something beyond book-jacket summaries and promised them a chance at a passing grade on their blue-book essays, along with the promise that they could still spend time at the Homecoming Parade.

Whether by design or happenstance, the CliffsNotes color code has apparently become the standard indicator for the "down and dirty" primer toward any subject. One needn't travel far in any bookstore to find a "Dummies Guide" to just about anything. The cover colors are black and yellow. Both are owned by John Wiley & Sons.

The sculpture by Claes Oldenburg and Coosje van Bruggen, *Torn Notebook*, lies just behind the welcoming center for the UNL campus, facing the rest of downtown Lincoln. It most likely has no intentional tie to this city's most ubiquitous contribution to student studies in the last half of the last century, but one cannot avoid making a connection. The oversize spiral notebook welcomes prospective students and parents with a vision of daily notes lost, contorted as though chewed on by a dog, or dropped from a backpack into uncaring game-day foot traffic, or torn in frustration and anguish by someone who simply ran out of study time.

Number 1

Nebraskans like their world flat. They like their roads straight, their fields in corn, and their four-legged critters bovine. It's a rather unified place, and the epicenter of this monoculture is Memorial Stadium in Lincoln on game day. That would be University of Nebraska football game day, the autumn Saturdays when I-80 is bumper-to-bumper as 80,000 single-minded Nebraskans convene in a crowd that's larger than all but two of the state's cities. Sure enough, they are uniformly clad in Husker red to celebrate Husker Nation, a quasi-mythical land where young, strapping farm kids are trained to beat the bejesus out of every other squad in the country. Football is the only serious sport in Nebraska. Everything else might as well be intramural, powder-puff badminton.

Even when the University of Nebraska's phenomenal Amazonian women's volleyball team wins a couple of national championships in a row, Nebraskans still talk football. It's proof positive that there's no room in this state for two of anything. This even holds true in politics, where Nebraska is the only state in the union with a unicameral (one-house) legislature. And the legislature is officially a nonpartisan body, so there aren't even two parties duking it out in the state capitol. Just another example of the low-key, pragmatic approach to things here.

It's not that Nebraskans don't plan for diversity; they just don't exhibit it. Nebraska politicos demonstrated an awareness of the possibility of disagreement when it became one of only two states in the country that allows for a split of its Electoral College votes. And until the Presidential election in 2008, Nebraskans had never split their electoral votes because the popular votes are generally so overwhelmingly one-sided. When faced with the choice between a candidate for change and a maverick in 2008, voters in Congressional District 2 (Omaha and environs) went for Obama. Otherwise, most elections have been fairly unanimous. Even when Nebraskans elected a woman as governor, it was when both major political party candidates were women. Now that's variety, Nebraska style.

★ ★

Shouldn't this be painted black and yellow?

The artists considered many images for Lincoln prior to choosing the notebook—they considered a field of popping corn, a giant hot dog, or roller skates. Bet the National Roller Skating Museum is still mourning that decision.

The sculpture is on the northeast corner of 12th and Q Streets.

Oh, Zero!
Lincoln

> Come, Nebraska, sing and dance with me—
> Come lovers of Lincoln and Omaha,
> hear my soft voice at last . . .
>
> Allen Ginsberg, Wichita Vortex Sutra

Lincolnians, or Lincolnites, or Lincolnesians (or whatever toponym and demonym researchers call them) are happy to tell visitors of the special nature of their main thoroughfare through town, O Street. It runs east-west through town, with N Street running parallel to the south, and P

Lincoln's main street is O.

★ ★

Street to the north. No, the first transcontinental highway, the Lincoln Highway, did not come through Lincoln. This particular stretch of road is cited by locals as the longest, straightest main street in the world.

It's hard to tell how the claim is substantiated—the O Street trip through east and west Lincoln city limits hardly seems all that impressive—but judging by the way that cities are historically built, next to a river or on an historic cowpath, it may be possible that the 10.5-mile length is sufficient to make the claim. If, on the other hand, locals mean to include the entire length of the straight road, it starts 42 miles to the east in an adjoining county and lies 13 miles to the west where it changes from pavement to gravel as O Street. The road goes

The Future Is Now

Toward the end of the Atomic Age, when bomb shelters and "duck and cover" education waned, and as the crew of the Apollo mission cruised to the moon for an historic walk, a one-hit-wonder folk-rock duo from Lincoln made its mark on the rock-and-roll charts with a song called "In the Year 2525 (Exordium and Terminus)." The song hit number 1 on the Billboard Hot 100 in early July 1969 and stayed there for an incredible six weeks; it topped the charts in the UK in August. According to a Billboard special report, *Forty Years of the Top 40*, the song was the biggest one-hit wonder in music history by selling twenty million copies worldwide in 1969.

The last dated verse goes like this:
In the year 9595,
I'm kinda wonderin' if Man is gonna be alive.
He's taken everything this old Earth can give,
and he ain't put back nothing.

for another 15 miles until it finally veers northwest. That gives the main street room to expand with a growing Lincoln to a full 80 miles.

Beat poet Allen Ginsberg made several references to Nebraska and to downtown Lincoln in his less-famous-than-"Howl" anti-war poem, "Wichita Vortex Sutra." In that poem, Ginsberg referenced Lincoln's main street as Zero Street. Much has changed in Lincoln, much remains the same. The reader can decide if the exhortations against Vietnam in that 1966 poem have any relevance to the wars America fights today and if the sentiments, like the long, straight drive on Zero Street, are on target or of little value.

Fair Advertising
Lincoln

The Nebraska State Fair has struggled to find its place in the summer sun, to keep its attendance numbers up in a world where residents and potential attendees can now see more things and try more foods in their own neighborhoods than they can find at the state fair. For years, attendees who once found reason to crowd together in unconditioned buildings have been staying away in droves.

In 2001 the State Fair Board hired a firm to develop an attention-getting billboard campaign to draw more people to the fair. A Lincoln firm developed award-winning ads that drew national attention from CNN, *USAToday*, and *Adweek* magazine, and garnered news coverage in other states. The theme? "Nebraska State Fair. Strangely Fun." The ad copy, with its suggestions to "Engage in heavy petting," or "See bands you thought were dead," and observations such as "The only place where you pay to throw up" or "If you can put it on a stick, it's food," generated some negative reactions among a few vocal locals.

Whimsy and good wordsmithing will often raise the ire of the "Heartland values" crowd, especially if directed toward institutions now based more on ritual than reason. But if you have been to state fairs from Nebraska to Alaska, you'll understand the ads ring true.

★ ★

Trivia

In the 1962 Doris Day and Rock Hudson movie *Lover Come Back,* cosmopolitan New York advertising man Jerry Webster (Hudson) gets to know freshly transplanted Nebraskan Carol Templeton (Day):

Webster (incredulously): "You mean they have advertising in Nebraska?"

Templeton: "Yes. Of course, it was a small agency, in Omaha."

The ad campaign, along with a serious infusion of cash in the following years, has started to bring in bigger crowds. Even so, city fathers and the state legislature have worked out a plan to relocate the fair to a more central location in Grand Island. As of this writing, the fair runs at the State Fairgrounds in Lincoln from late August to early September. Wherever it is when you go, enjoy yourself. And remember to wear old shoes.

Priapic-upied
Lincoln

> All art is erotic.
> Adolph Loos

Nebraskans love their national championships. Even without billboards, stadium marquees, and innumerable T-shirts and caps to remind them, any Lincoln resident can recite the years their beloved Cornhuskers won national football championships.

Through the years, these contests have created among hometown fans a low-level antagonism toward frequent combatants in Oklahoma, Colorado, and Florida.

★ ★

Given such competitiveness, how is it possible that capital city residents did not raise a howl of protest when, in 2003, the Florida state capital received the most popular votes as the "Most Phallic Building in the World" by *Cabinet Magazine*? One always wonders about voting irregularities in Florida, after all.

Surely the Nebraska state capital deserves the title, or at least equal billing. Consider the conflicted symbol of Nebraska atop the state capitol, *The Sower*. Even after *The Sower's* well-publicized scrubbing and refurbishing a few years ago, the Nebraska advisory panel to the US Mint for the design of the Nebraska State Quarter spurned *The Sower* profile from a short list of Nebraska quarter image contenders. It seems they thought this Nebraska icon could become the butt of some jokes. "What is he doing with his hand in his pants, anyway?" "What makes his crotch seem so, ahem, large?" The quarter

Nebraska, a state of excitement. Honestly, we're just happy to see you.

committee uses a common standard for a decision in this college football–crazed state: that Nebraska quarter backs should be above reproach.

The Sower stands high above the once-virgin prairies with legs astride a massive shaft that connects it to the chamber from which the laws of Nebraska are conceived and born. He has since 1934 cupped his hand to spread his seed over the fertile fruited plains northwest of Lincoln. *The Sower* symbolizes both the productive agrarian past and germinating hope of a bountiful future. Why isn't this guy smiling?

As lofty as *The Sower* is, it is not mentioned nearly as often as the capitol spire, that (dare we say) compensatory column that provides the signature look for the Nebraska State Capitol. The capitol is introduced to newcomers as the Penis of the Plains in spite of several architectural notes that stress its unique character as the only art deco state capitol in the United States. One could consider *The Sower's* second billing to that of the capitol unfortunate, a bit of bad luck. Or perhaps it represents an uncanny ability to speak to the masses.

Even before there was a Nebraska, Nebraskans knew the importance of a penis. Most famous of the western expansion phallic markers is the natural western Nebraska signpost, Chimney Rock. Long before Europeans arrived, the natives had tagged this prominent protrusion *Heh^aka Che*, or Elk Penis. Early pioneers used the phrase Prick of the Prairie. It served as a guidepost for the wayfaring traveler, a pillar of certainty on the otherwise unbroken expanse of prairie in the middle of the mysterious and occasionally unwelcoming plains. And thus was this pillar of tradition formed for generations to come.

Perhaps it was this cultural memory that guided the early leaders of the state to embrace the phallic symbol and to erect their own when this third state capitol was conceived. Rather than trying to hide the coarse colloquialisms, perhaps Nebraska ought to compete with Florida for the title of America's Most Priapic State.

Trivia

The goldenrod (*Soldiago gigantea*) was declared the state flower in 1895. As noted in an article written by Ida Brockman, "It has a long season, and nothing could better represent the hardy endurance of Nebraska's pioneers." It also serves as a great candidate for a team name: the Golden Rods.

Rat Olympics

Lincoln

In 1974 Nebraska Wesleyan University psychology professor Dr. Marty Klein introduced as part of his Behavioral Learning Principles course a hands-on lesson for the students. What Dr. Klein began in 1974 is essentially what is done today, and is distinctive from most other schools' use of computer models.

Each student is assigned a rat early in the semester. Throughout the semester the students apply the knowledge gained during lectures about types of behavior reinforcement to their rats. The students direct the rats to respond to cues in order to learn new behaviors. In December both students and rats demonstrated their semester gains in knowledge in a final demonstration project originally dubbed the Rat Olympics. The rats seek honors in hurdles, weight lifting, long jump, tight rope, and rope climb competition.

The Rat Olympic track events and feats of strength became a big hit when in 2001 the competition expanded its audience outside of class, drawing other students, teachers, parents, and members of the community to the annual competition. But twenty-nine years after the games began, the United States Olympic Committee legal team did some armchair coaching of their own. The USOC told Nebraska Wesleyan in a January 2003 letter that it would sue if university officials

★ ★

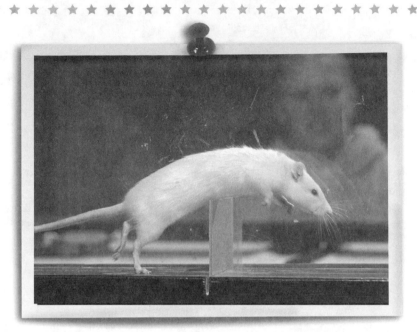

Going for the gold! Courtesy of Nebraska Wesleyan University

continued to use "Olympics" as the name for their class competition. The USOC asserted that it owns exclusive rights to the word "Olympics."

"We expressed our displeasure with the name, and the negative connotation it had being associated with the Olympic brand," said a lawyer quoted by the *Chronicle of Higher Education.*

The Wesleyan psychology department took the request in stride, deciding to ask for suggestions to rename the competition. More than 200 people from over half of the United States and five foreign countries suggested alternatives, including Rat Races and Iron Rat Competition, prior to an official change to the Xtreme Rat Challenge.

The best adage for this tale might be "it's an ill wind that doesn't blow anyone any good," or "there's no such thing as bad publicity." After the hypersensitive USOC law squad issued their "request," even more publicity for the program occurred. Since the event first went public in 2001, publicity for the event has been offered by multiple local television stations, ESPN, the Discovery Channel, the BBC, the *Wall Street Journal*, *Discover* magazine, and most recently on the *Modern Marvels* show on the History Channel.

The point of contact at NWU is Dr. Marilyn Petro, an assistant professor of psychology; call (402) 465-2429, e-mail mpetro@nebr wesleyan.edu, or go to www.nebrwesleyan.edu/depts/psyc/xtreme.htm.

Bumper Art
Lincoln

Chrome means cool for people of a certain age. There was a time when designers put fins on the backs of cars and spent a great deal of care designing a front grill so laden with chrome that the lights of roadside streetlamps reflected off the plating in 50-miles-per-hour side-showers like a full set of 1970s disco balls on wheels.

Over time many different influences forced changes on the auto-motive manufacturing market, and chrome dropped out of favor in the industry. And chrome-plated bumpers, hubcaps, and other car parts moved off production-line vehicles and faded away from high-ways to grow in number in automobile graveyards.

Frisbee Panned

Numbers of stories exist about the origins of the famous flying toy the Frisbee. According to students of Middlebury College in Vermont, a group of their students who were attending a fraternity meeting in Lincoln in 1938 found entertainment by flying a pan in classic flying disc fashion. They have even erected a statue on their campus to celebrate the art. But while they may have played, the people who live here claim to have somehow inspired the action.

★ ★

What better use of otherwise wasted and shiny, extremely slow corroding material than to find another use for it? Loi Vo of Lincoln Industries (formerly Lincoln Plating) does just that. He took his talent for working with chrome-plated materials, mixed in a healthy dose of creativity, and created a specialized art portfolio of chrome-plated metal sculptures.

His employers at Lincoln Industries took a liking to his work, and have an eagle on display at the main offices just off Capitol Drive. And Vo's works can be found among those with eclectic tastes around town. Pepe's Restaurant, for example, has displayed different pieces inside and out that Vo has done—from grasshoppers to space shuttles.

Once you identify Vo's work, you can find several installations around town—putting a real shine on recycling.

Shiny baubles make me happy, make me feel fine.

May the Best Man Win

In this case, the man was a woman. In 1986 Nebraska became the first state in which both major parties fielded women as candidates for governor when State Treasurer Kay Orr ran against Democrat and former Lincoln Mayor Helen Boosalis. As a result of the election, Kay Orr became the first Republican woman in the nation elected as governor, and to date she has been the only woman who served as governor of Nebraska.

The first woman-versus-woman race happened in a traditionally conservative state that had never before fielded a woman as a candidate for governor.

The contest was civil, never reaching the level of mano a mano combat.

Food Fancy, Not Fancy Food

Lincoln

One doesn't need to look too far in a crowd of Nebraskans to come to an inescapable conclusion: Nebraskans love food.

And while this Flyover Country is famous as the source of the best cuts of meat available in the country, it's a sad but little-known fact that those same cuts that earned the state its well-deserved reputation as a place to grow great beef are mostly sent out of state to top-of-the-line restaurants around the world.

The sad fact is that the average Nebraskan who doesn't raise beef for a living also doesn't eat the best and most expensive cuts.

That fact has not been lost on the food intellects who live here. Omaha claims to have the restaurant that invented the Reuben sandwich. But that was a singular, inspired genius. Nebraska's number one

Haven't seen this in a store shelf near you?
That's because a "cornana" would change
forever what it means to be a Cornhusker.
Craig McNiven

industry is raising food, but its number two is food processing. While
the muses may visit chefs on occasion, good ol' American know-how
and engineering has put researchers to work along with the food pro-
cessors in order to invent new, affordable foods for the masses.

A food genius at the Swanson company in Omaha invented the TV
dinner, that affordable frozen fare first formed in foil partitions and
cooked in an oven, back when shows were broadcast live, black and
white, and you took turns getting up to change the channel.

But leave it to the food engineers at the University of Lincoln to
come up with one of the greatest inventions of modern food processing: pressed meat. Yummy! In 1972 Professor Roger Mandigo

received money from the National Pork Producers Council and created a process to make "restructured meat patties." This process is what lies behind the tasty formed meat treats like the McRib (ribs without the hassle of bones!) and boneless chicken "wings."

Lick It and Stick It
Omaha, Boys Town Suburb

Boys Town was 10 miles outside of Omaha when it moved to its current location in 1921. Today Omaha has sprawled out to include it and acres of other former farmland for another 10 miles. In 1938 Boys Town achieved national notoriety when Spencer Tracy and Mickey Rooney starred in a movie of the same name.

In 1953, when "snail mail" was the norm and a philatelic fascination seemed a reasonable hobby, a group of Boys Town residents

That's Heavy, Man!

In 2005 *Men's Fitness* magazine partnered with the research organization the Princeton Review for the first-ever list of fattest and fittest colleges. The University of Nebraska at Omaha was judged to be the eleventh fattest in the nation.

In contrast, host city Omaha is one of the fittest towns in the United States. In 2004 *Men's Fitness* magazine ranked Omaha as the eleventh fittest city in America; in 2005 Omaha was only the sixteenth fittest; in 2006 Omaha slipped to the twenty-fifth fittest; in 2007 Omaha climbed back to twelfth; inching upward again in 2008 to eleventh and making it into the top ten in 2009 at number nine.

★ ★

decided to create a stamp ball. Beginning with a nubbin of an eraser at its core, it took the combined effort of multiple contributors a couple of years and an undetermined amount of spittle or glue to put together around 4,655,000 canceled stamps into what became a 600-pound, 100-inch-circumference ball of stamps. When done, they lacquered it up and called it good. A Ripley's Believe It or Not! column, displayed with the ball, called attention to their feat in 1955 and attracted crowds.

You can easily find more than one "world's largest ball of twine," but you won't find another contender for the largest ball of stamps

So . . . what have you done philately?

Trivia

The four story, thirty-four-room Joslyn Castle on five acres at Thirty-ninth and Davenport in Omaha's Gold Coast neighborhood was referred to as Lynhurst by its original residents when it was built in 1903. It included a specially made bathtub for the pet dog, still viewable today.

Cleanliness is next to godliness, little doggy. Hop in.

★ ★

title. For over fifty years the competition simply hasn't existed—as evidenced by the fact that the ball hasn't grown since its creation except for the addition of a four-cent commemorative Father Flanigan stamp in 1986. So certain are they of their stamp ball supremacy, visitors are not allowed to bring in their favorite stamps to grow the ball, not a lick.

The World's Largest Stamp ball is displayed in front of a splashy stamp mural backdrop that's nothing to spit at in the Leon Myers Stamp Center, a philatelic museum within the Boys Town Visitors Center. It's open Monday through Friday from 8:00 a.m. to 4:00 p.m., Saturday from 9:00 a.m. to 4:00 p.m., and Sunday from 11:00 a.m. to 4:00 p.m. For more information, call (888) 556-5123 or go to www.boystown.org/Products/Pages/Stamps.aspx.

Attack Plaque
Omaha, Dundee neighborhood

From November 1944 until April 1945, Japan launched approximately 9,000 bomb-carrying helium balloons, called fire balloons or fugos, in an attack on the United States. Experts estimate that close to 1,000 made it to North America; about 300 were actually accounted for. The most recent one was found in Alaska in 1992.

When US authorities first learned of the attack, they worked with the press to keep it quiet until a family in Oregon was killed by one. Japan claimed that fugo-started firestorms swept the United States and caused numerous casualties. Never trust the government in a time of war, no matter which side you are on.

One fire balloon made it over 6,000 miles to Dundee, which was then on the outskirts of Omaha. A plaque that commemorates the event is on a building on the south side of Underwood Street, just west of Fiftieth. It reads:

IN THE SKY OVER 50TH AND UNDERWOOD, A JAPANESE BALLOON BOMB
EXPLODED ON APRIL 18, 1945. THE INCENDIARY DEVICE FLARED BRIGHTLY IN
THE NIGHT, BUT CAUSED NO DAMAGE.

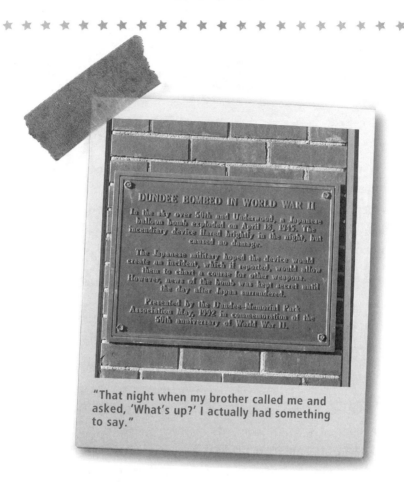

"That night when my brother called me and asked, 'What's up?' I actually had something to say."

THE JAPANESE MILITARY HOPED THE DEVICE WOULD CREATE AN INCI-DENT, WHICH IF REPORTED, WOULD ALLOW THEM TO CHART A COURSE FOR OTHER WEAPONS. HOWEVER, NEWS OF THE BOMB WAS KEPT SECRET UNTIL THE DAY AFTER JAPAN SURRENDERED.

WWII was a time of inventive aerial wartime attacks. It's too bad the US military didn't get to finish at least one of their secret weapon schemes. "Project X-Ray" planned to use about a million bats strapped to incendiary devices in order to dive-bomb Japan. Batty idea? Hardly. When these bat bombs were tested, they unintention-ally torched a military facility in New Mexico.

★ ★

Two to Tango

The most notable air attack of WWII had its beginnings in a hangar, Building D, which is now a recreational facility at Offutt Air Force Base in Bellevue just south of Omaha. It was there that the Enola Gay and Bock's Car were fitted for their mission to Japan. These two bombers were the first and only aircraft to drop atomic weapons used in a military action.

It's a Small World, After All

Omaha

Do you recall the trivia game called the Six Degrees of Kevin Bacon? Players with a good deal of cinematic knowledge were challenged with the name of an actor or actress. In order to meet the challenge, the player had to name films in which that actor and another had appeared, and in six or fewer such pairings go from the challenge name to Kevin Bacon. For example, if the challenge was Omaha-born Nick Nolte, an appropriate reply would demonstrate that Nolte's Bacon Number = 2. (As a matter of fact, all of the Omaha-born actors appear to have a Bacon number of 2, including Marlon Brando, Henry Fonda, and Fred Astaire.)

Nick Nolte and Margo Martindale appeared in *Paris, je t'aime*, released in 2006.

Margo Martindale and Kevin Bacon appeared in *Rails & Ties*, released in 2007.

The game was popularized as example of the concept that you, dear reader, are no more than six connections from anyone else in the world. It's the somewhat counterintuitive view that even though there are more and more people on the planet, there is now a greater likelihood of social connection between any two people, not less. More people with access to travel and communication mean more social networks. More social networks mean more opportunities to know someone who has a friend in common. Or, "I have friends who have friends." Eventually, some mathematician suggested that you are never more than six connections away from anyone.

It's a comforting thought for individuals who worry about getting lost in a crowd.

Omaha had a significant role in the development of the six degrees concept.

The notion that there might be a small number of connections to link up everyone in the world has been around for some time as a theoretical mathematical construct. But Harvard social psychologist Stanley Milgram set out to find the number separating Americans in a landmark experiment he conducted back in the late 1960s. He randomly chose residents in Omaha as a starting point in a communication chain. These people were asked to forward a letter to a designated target person in Massachusetts if they knew that person; if they did not know the intended target, they were to send the information to someone who might know the person with the same instructions.

It's as though the underlying assumption in the original study was that Omaha is as far from the rest of the world (meaning "the coast"?) as anyone could get, both geographically and socially. Is it any wonder that Nebraskans are suspicious of East Coast university professorial types?

Dr. Milgram's studies found that the average connection between two people unknown to each other in Omaha and Boston is six. The importance of the study was not the number of connections, which has been argued since, but the fact that everyone is connected— even to people in Omaha! Dr. Milgram referred to the probability of personal linkages as the "Small World Problem," but did not use the well-known phrase "six degrees of separation." That phrase arose

★ ★

The University of Nebraska at Omaha claims to have more alumni who are general officers than any other institution in the country save West Point.

with the above-mentioned trivia game and other popular uses that were sparked by the small-world concept.

What is not known, interestingly, is which Omahans were in the study. Perhaps you know one?

Malcolm X-ing
Omaha

Malcolm Little was born May 19, 1925, at the University of Nebraska Hospital. The next year his family moved away from his first home in Omaha to Milwaukee in part because of threats made by the local Ku Klux Klan.

Malcolm eventually changed his name to El-Hajj Malik El-Shabazz but was more popularly known as Malcolm X. He was assassinated in New York in 1965.

Alex Haley wrote *The Autobiography of Malcolm X*, identified by *Time Magazine* as one of the ten most important books of the twentieth century; Spike Lee adapted the book in his film, *Malcolm X*. Historian Robin D.G. Kelley wrote, "Malcolm X has been called many things: Pan-Africanist, father of Black Power, religious fanatic, closet conservative, incipient socialist, and a menace to society . . . Malcolm has become a sort of tabula rasa, or blank slate, on which people of different positions can write their own interpretations of his politics and legacy. Chuck D of the rap group Public Enemy and Supreme

Court Justice Clarence Thomas can both declare Malcolm X their hero." Given that, many have found it curious that the local effort to memorialize Omaha's connection to Malcolm X hasn't generated more support.

Call it "the X-ing."

★ ★

A state historical marker exists at the first home for Malcolm X. The house was torn down in 1965, the location was listed on the National Register of Historic Places in 1984, and the state historic marker was added in 1987 and can be found at 3448 Pinkney Street.

Many structures have been built during the reurbanization of downtown Omaha for which the naming of Malcolm X has been suggested. The most recent is the new city landmark and as yet un-named Omaha-Council Bluffs Missouri River pedestrian bridge. The naming of this bridge has not yet been set, but could there be a better honor for a native son and name for the river crossing than Malcolm X-ing?

Spotted Past
Omaha

It sounds extraordinarily insensitive, especially given the context of the times in which it appeared. After all, *Gone With the Wind* was published in 1936 and released as a movie in 1939. And it's hard to imagine now that the border signs that today welcome travelers to Nebraska's "Good Life" in the late 1930s and through the 1940s instead announced Nebraska as the WHITE SPOT OF THE NATION.

The phrase was a marketing pitch intended to attract businesses to relocate. "White Spot" was intended as a brand for Nebraska's unique tax structure at the time. Nebraska was the "White Spot of the Nation" because it had no state income tax, no sales tax, no luxury taxes, and no state debt, and yet had drivable roads and competitive schools. The state constitution prohibited the state from issuing state bonds. The unicameral legislature governed with a mind-set that every building, road, and piece of equipment owned by the state should be without debt.

Democratic governor Robert Cochran made considerable noise plugging Nebraska's business-friendly tax environment to all who would listen. The Omaha Chamber of Commerce, then and always on the prowl for a way to publicize local prowess, raised enough money to run some advertisements in *Time Magazine* that used a white map of Nebraska centrally located in a black map of the rest of the borderless forty-eight states.

Other local economic groups and newspapers, buttressed by antitax-minded citizens, helped give the campaign legs with license plate add-ons, border signs, and other advertising gewgaws using the phrase and the map.

The campaign is credited with luring five businesses to Omaha; the larger marketing impact was to reinforce a view of Nebraskans as loathe to spend public funds and unconvinced by arguments about progressive tax policies.

After all, everyone knows tax policy has nothing to do with race.

Proud to be tax-free.
Library of Congress

★ ★

A Mediocre Defense

Omaha

Nebraska has contributed its fair share of memorable expressions to the national political lexicon, including William Jennings Bryan's Cross of Gold speech and Standing Bear's simple observation at the trial to determine whether a Native American is a human: "This hand is not the same color as yours but if I pierce it, I shall feel pain. The blood that will flow from mine will be the same color as yours. I am a man. The same God made us both."

The depth and breadth of notable Nebraska phrases exceeds the scope of this book. But one contribution to political discourse

Mediocracy in memoriam.

deserves a mention precisely because the people who write such books are likely to ignore it.

In 1970 Roman Hruska, US senator from Nebraska, gained notoriety with his extemporaneous defense of a nominee to the US Supreme Court. The Senate majority was at odds with White House choice G. Harrold Carswell, citing his "incredibly undistinguished career as an attorney and jurist . . . [as] an affront to the Supreme Court" and arguing that the Senate should not let its standards " . . . fall to the low level suggested by the present nominee."

Enter Omaha native Hruska, the ranking Republican on the Senate Judiciary Committee and Carswell's principal defender. Hruska stayed on script until he left the Senate Chamber. It was there that a reporter asked for his view about the charge that Carswell was mediocre. Senator Hruska tried his best at turning lemons into lemonade when he said, "Well, even if he were mediocre, there are a lot of mediocre judges and people and lawyers. They are entitled to a little representation, aren't they, and a little chance? We can't have all Brandeises and Frankfurters and Cardozos and stuff like that there."

Hruska's defense proved fatal to the nomination and provided fodder for a discussion that continues today.

Now most complaints of congressional representation are not because of mediocre intellect—no one thinks legislators set their goals that high. Meritocracy may be the complaint on extremist talk shows, but mediocracy is the norm.

World's Cleanest Airport
Omaha

Midwesterners have always been rightly proud of their cleanliness. Maybe it's all the fussy Scandinavians and Germans who settled here back when real estate agents dealt in sod houses. Imagine how tough it would be to keep the place spick-and-span when earthworms live in the ceiling and your kitchen floor is susceptible to spring potholes and occasional twisters in July.

★ ★

Now That's Leadership!

"Being a colorless conservative is what Nebraska is all about."
—Governor Charles Thone, *Lincoln Star*, January 1, 1983

"It is not that Nebraskans are necessarily opposed to progress, they just don't want to pay for it."
—Governor James J. Exon, *Lincoln Evening Journal*, November 4, 1970

"I don't think about things I don't think about."
—William Jennings Bryan, three-time presidential candidate, at the so-called Scopes Monkey Trial.

These daily challenges created a culture of tidiness in Nebraska, and nowhere is the tradition celebrated with more unabashed pride than at Omaha's Eppley Airfield. There are probably other airports where the polished floor surfaces shine as brightly and the bathrooms succumb to as much disinfectant. But nowhere else is an airport's direct marketing of its cleanliness so . . . well, direct.

We can't speak for the women's restrooms, but the "World's Cleanest Airport" slogan is prominently displayed in each and every urinal at Eppley. It's printed on the plastic strainers that prevent coastal visitors from clogging the plumbing with gum or chewing tobacco. In fact, to see that message while staring into a urinal automatically inspires guilt, and in this heavily Catholic state, it will make you feel right at home.

A note for those wondering about the man for whom this airport was named, Eugene Eppley. Mr. Eppley was a regional hotelier who lived in the Fontanelle Hotel in Omaha. He was a noted philanthropist and supporter of artists such as the not-very-well-known-at-the-time

Grant Woods, the Iowan who painted the iconic *American Gothic*. Eppley commissioned Woods to paint murals in several of his hotels, including the work known as The Corn Room. Yes, it's true; even in metropolitan Nebraska, even at the spot where the fastest transport touches down, there is a tie to corn.

The Omaha Airport Authority and Eppley Airfield are located at 4501 Abbott Drive, Suite 2300. For more information, call (402) 661-8000.

We aim to please. You aim, too, please.

Iowa Insurgency

There's a fun, if confusing, bit of geography to be found when traveling the 5 miles south from the Omaha Eppley Airfield directly to the heart of downtown Omaha. About 2 miles after passing a rather large and well-manicured landscaping feature welcoming the traveler to Omaha, there is another sign on the roadway downtown that welcomes travelers to Iowa. Iowa is a state that by all rights should be to the east of Nebraska, across the Missouri River.

When the state boundaries were declared years ago, there was an oxbow in the river, a hernia-like extrusion of Iowa into Nebraska. In 1877 a flood straightened out the river-way after the borders had been set. The US Supreme Court decided the land belonged to Iowa. That's how part of Iowa ended up west of part of eastern Nebraska.

Iowa has had much more fun with this than has Nebraska. There is no sign notifying the traveler bound for Omaha that they are back in Nebraska once they have gotten into Iowa. From the signage alone, one might conclude that Omaha is really in Iowa.

The WELCOME TO IOWA sign provides a source of constant irritation to the larger and easily offended Omaha. When it comes up in conversation between neighboring mayors or councilmen, you can sense a tension of ill-mannered siblings sparring over the rules of the line dividing a shared space.

Simply ignore them and enjoy the view, just as you would ignore the squabbling of two kids in the backseat of your car.

Palindromaha
Omaha

In *The Newton Boys*, a 1998 film with mixed reviews, the following exchange took place between Willis Newton, played by Matthew McConaughey, and Louise Brown, played by Julianna Margulies:

Willis: "So, what's a fella do in Omaha?" Louise: "Well, he could chew gum."

Perhaps if he were a bit more ambitious, he could seek some mental diversions such as creating palindromes, those phrases that read the same forward and backward. A few oft-used examples of palindromes have been published over the years, but thanks to the Internet and computer programming, it has gotten a little easier to find or create them.

As you might expect, many of the Omaha-related palindromes are exclamatory in nature. The challenge lies with trying to think of places they could actually be used.

For a matchmaking service:

Aha, Monica met a mate, Mac, in Omaha.

Perhaps this explains why the Eppley airport is so clean:

Aha! More vomit, Tim, over Omaha!

Dena's utterance when waking up to find it's her turn to drive cross-country:

"Aha," moaned Dena, "Omaha."

E-mail reply to an observation by the tour operator that for once while riding the paddlewheel boat downriver, it wasn't mooned by either a boatload of carousers or by people on shore:

Re: No Omaha Mooner

A reelection campaign tagline for a telegenic mayor:

Ah, a model led Omaha.

A slogan for a local astronomy club:

Rats, no Omaha moon-star.

What palindrome-interested rural Nebraskans say when suggesting a trip to the big city:

"Slap a ham on Omaha, pals."

Unfortunately, longtime eatery, Mr. C's is now closed. Perhaps this is better used as dialogue overheard in a mystery, where the hero needs to figure out what the C stands for:

"Aha, Monica! A 'C' in Omaha."

Any dialogue the Omaha Visitors Bureau has with Moses that emphasizes the great things about Omaha:

"Aha, Moses—Omaha!"

What Mr. T says to answer the following question: "What is the name of a sponge, an over-actor, and a town in Nebraska?"

"Loofa, ham, Omaha, fool!"

Hobbit Hole at the Old Folks Home

Omaha

Tucked behind an assisted living high-rise on South Tenth Street is a low, igloo-shaped structure of pocked and piled stones cemented together. Strands of ivy conceal it with an air of mystery. Open the door and you are welcomed by a musty smell of abandonment, but votive candles and small religious cards suggest the Grotto, as it is known, still serves a purpose.

The Grotto apparently dates back to the 1920s, when St. Joseph Hospital occupied the lot next door. A priest wanted those who visited the sick to have a nearby retreat for prayer and reflection. In his spare time, the priest gathered rocks one by one until he had enough to build this odd little chapel. The skylights are overgrown, and even when the sun is shining directly at the door, the uneven rock walls of the single room give occupants a definite sense that they are in an underground cave.

No one today knows much about the origins of this little hidey-hole. It's one of those places that is relatively easy to find if you go looking for it but hides in plain sight in a green space peninsula protruding into adjacent parking lots.

★ ★

It could be a shrine to Middle Earth.

While you're prowling around, take a look at the original archway entrance to St. Joe's Hospital. It's immediately east of the Grotto and is an attractive hand-carved remnant dating back to 1892.

To find it, you need to go to the intersection of Tenth and Dorcas Streets, then head east to the north entrance of the parking lot.

The door is open. Go with a friend.

Swollen with Pride

Omaha

Back when body piercings were the rage, when Garrison Keillor made mention of a metal-adorned teen as someone who "looked like they fell into a tackle box," twenty-one-year-old Omaha resident Matt

Brown set the record for most body piercings in one day with 171. He beat the previous record of 102 by having tattoo artist Joe Smith put all but 10 into his arms. His red and puffy arms bore testament to his 2001 endurance to pain.

Parents have for years chastised and derided new youthful fashion customs, especially those that yield lasting marks, either by ink or scar tissue. Who knows what his parents might have said to young Mr. Brown? A good parent knows that time is on their side, and if they are patient, they can have the quiet satisfaction of embarrassing their kids, even if they can't change their minds.

The current Guinness World Record for most piercings in one session is now at 1,015, set in March 2006. Wow. A number that high makes it seem like Matt wasn't really trying when he got 171.

Do you suppose that Matt received a copy of the edition of the *Guinness World Record* book from his family and friends with the new record? Can you imagine the conversation with the previous puncture champ about the long-lasting sense of accomplishment? Or about the many benefits of having 160 pairs of holes in his arms? Is his nickname now Pierce?

3

Southeast

*T*he southeastern part of the state is where Nebraska inserts
itself into a notch formed by Missouri and Kansas. People here
like to refer to this part of the country as the tristate area.
It's here where Wild Bill Hickok shot his first victim, where Arbor Day
began, and where early Nebraskans turned a territory into a state.
When much of the westward expansion began and grew, it was here
where impatient pioneers gave up their travel and stayed, figuring that
sod-busting and cholera would be better than moving any farther west.
Who would say they were wrong?

Some of the state's more odious modern crimes were carried out
here—and in this context the term *odious* is measured by whether the
crimes became fodder for Hollywood movies. More on that later.

Just a note about the Huskers: The University of Nebraska lies just
north of Husker Holler, in the westernmost county of the SubUrbane
Sprawl. Thanks in large measure to the residents of Husker Holler
and other parts of the state, a thriving cottage industry in tacky red-
and-white imported textiles and plastics was spawned. The interested
traveler will find Husker icons at practically every homestead along
the highway, and variations of official University of Nebraska–Lincoln
scarlet-and-cream colored shrines in almost every home. Somebody
is making big dollars from the free-spending fanaticism of Husker
football. In this part of the country, Huskerism and hucksterism wear
clothes cut from the same red-and-white cloth. Newcomers to the state

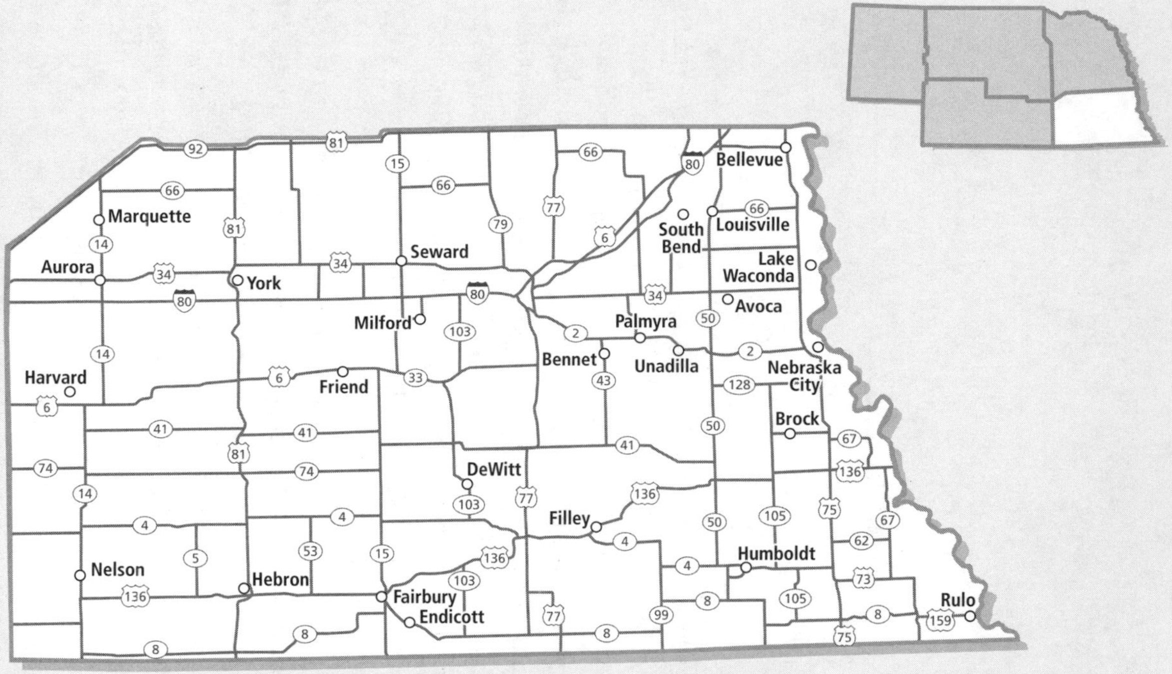
Bellevue
Louisville
South Bend
Lake Waconda
Avoca
Palmyra
Unadilla
Nebraska City
Bennet
Brock
Seward
Milford
York
Marquette
Aurora
Harvard
Friend
DeWitt
Filley
Humboldt
Rulo
Fairbury
Endicott
Hebron
Nelson

Southeast

★ ★

would do well to learn key introductory phrases like "Go Big Red!" or "How 'bout them Huskers?" in order to insinuate themselves into local conversations.

The dells and gullies that pocket Husker Holler lie betwixt hills that are more rolling and much more densely planted with trees than those of the Sand Hills out in more western Nebraska. But not all of the woodland is as it seems, for the fabled Giant Marijuana Forest of Eastern Nebraska lies here. Its exact location cannot be mapped; it has a quality to it like the Lost Seven Cities of Gold, or Brigadoon, or Shangri-La. Those who visit it speak fondly of their visit but never seem to be able to retrace their steps. You have likely seen old post-cards of an oversize ear of corn being drawn by a team of horses, with captions like "A small harvest" or "We grow some real corn here." The local mythology says that marijuana grows so tall in Husker Holler that it has to be felled with a chainsaw for a successful harvest. It doesn't contain the chemicals of medicinal marijuana, and conse-quently, you can buy a cord of the stuff for about as much as a few grams of what you can buy at local high schools elsewhere in the county. But those dances around the nightly bonfires!

While marijuana grows in other parts of Nebraska, it's smoked more often in Husker Holler than other parts of the state, according to the Substance Abuse and Mental Health Services Administration (SAMHSA) and reported in their Substate Estimates from the 1999–2001 National Surveys on Drug Use and Health (NSDUH), which might attract just a little more attention if it were named the National Over-view of Drug Use and Health, or NO-DUH.

★ ★

Freeze Frame
Aurora

The Baby Boomers who slacked and socialized in the late '60s can vaguely recall from among memories of black light posters and lava lamps the pre-disco-ball dance floor sensation known as the strobe light. When the strobe light was turned on while dancers were doing the mashed potato, it gave anyone watching the contorting teens the sense that all the motion had been turned into a live-action flip book. When lights went off and the strobe light went on, a dance floor chorus of "Oh, wow, man" was sure to ensue among those with already confused temporal function. As use of the strobe light spread to more and more dance events across the country, so did an awareness that a part of our population suffers from photosensitive epilepsy, where exposure to strobe lighting can trigger seizures. Oops.

It was just another example of technological repurposing, which supports the notion that "Nothing is foolproof, because fools are so

Doc invented the art of capturing a kerplunk on film. Scott Butner

ingenious." The creation of the stroboscope was born of the genius of Nebraska-born Doc Edgerton, cited as one of the fifteen most influential inventors of the twentieth-century industrial revolution. The local boy who became Dr. Harold Edgerton also invented flash photography and side-scan sonar.

In recognition of their local son and with a belief that science can be fun, this small Nebraska community created a hands-on science center to honor the man. The Edgerton Explorit Center opened in 1995. A trip through the center will reward the curious with stop-action views suitable to this part of the country—well suited to the sense that no matter how fast the East and West Coasts volley changes to each other, here in the center things stand still.

A visitor will also be treated to one of Doc Edgerton's favorite traveling exhibits, the Double Piddler. This isn't a piddly single Piddler, it's a Double Piddler. Imagine two streams of liquid that fall toward the same point on the ground. (Guys, think of the phrase "crossing swords.") Now turn a strobe light on the two streams of liquid and turn off the surrounding light. If you are successful at adjusting the speed of the strobe flash, it will appear as though the droplets are standing still in midair. With careful adjustment, the droplets will look as though they are heading back upstream.

The Edgerton Explorit Center is located at 208 Sixteenth Street. For more information, call (402) 694-4032 or go to www.edgerton.org.

Duck Flopalotofit's a Winner
Avoca

Small towns in Nebraska have been getting smaller as the farms surrounding them have been getting larger. For those who are midway between harvesting and planting, the long nights and low temperatures can't be compensated by adding another set of channels on their satellite TV subscription.

Avoca found the best way to deal with the doldrums of winter in 1980 when it began the Avoca Duck Races.

★ ★

One can imagine the conversation that started it all.

"Cold enough for you?" the son asked his father as he joined him at the local tavern.

"Yup." His dad wasn't much for words.

"This town could use some excitement," said the young man, beginning another round in a friendly contest between himself and the bartender about who had the best idea to turn Avoca into a collegiate must-do road trip for the 12,000 women in attendance at the University of Nebraska campus about 40 miles distant. They both knew there must be some way to earn a spot on a rite-of-passage list, along with body surfing in the student section of a Husker football game while singing "There is No Place Like Nebraska."

"Maybe we could hold a beauty contest. A Nebraska Ice Queen?" posited the barkeep.

"How about a tractor pull on ice?" countered the youth.

The oldest of the three in the bar finally spoke up. "Here's what we're gonna do. First, we're gonna get us some ducks and head down to the . . . No, no, wait, wait." He looked at the tavern owner and said, "First thing we do is we get us some beer. Then we get some ducks and head down to the pond on the edge of town. It ought to be good and frozen by now . . . "

However the conversation went, the event was born and has grown to become an annual place to be and be seen for people throughout the region—bringing in several hundred ducks and duck jockeys from nearby states. Over 1,000 Quack-Off fans descend on this town of 270 in the middle of winter to drink beer, shiver in the cold, and howl at the sight of foolish friends and serious duck-tenders shouting at waddlers doing their best to race from one end of a flooded and frozen tennis court baseline to the other. Participants (both avian athlete and owner/trainer) are encouraged to arrive in costume, although anyone can enter the event for a mere $10. No duck? (What?! You don't have a duck?) No worries. For an additional

$5 you can rent one for the day. Training tips from fans and fellow trainers are free.

Some contestants spend more time working on their duck's name than on training it. A well-considered name takes about the same amount of time to develop as does the training; the difference is that drinking more beer seems to help duck naming while it tends to hinder duck training. The race announcer will give more air time to a well-named duck, a la Bart Simpson's calls to Moe's Bar (Ollie Tabooger) or the Car Talk Credits (Andy Zoff). Or choose your own inspiration—Quackulon the Destroyer and Quack Whore have been used. But notoriety won't win the race; it is usually a well-trained or very lucky duck that makes it into the next round.

The Quack-Off Races happen the third weekend in January, with proceeds given to the local volunteer fire department. And while not all of the coeds from nearby universities make a point to attend, many do make the trip. Hats off to the event planners at local taverns across the world.

Just duckin' around.

★ ★

An Undisclosed Location

Bellevue

September 11, 2001. You no doubt remember what you were doing that morning as the unbelievable scenes unfolded on our television screens and embedded themselves into the national consciousness.

As the national defense systems kicked into place, the Strategic Air Command at Offutt Air Force Base did the job it continuously trains to do.

While the national media stated more than once that the president's location was kept secret, those who watched the skies around Bellevue knew that President George W. Bush was in town. That's right: When the going gets scary, land the president in Flyover Country. Nobody will find him here.

There could have been one other reason for bringing the president to Offutt Air Force Base. Offutt serves as the home of the US Strategic Command (STRATCOM), which prior to June 1992 was known as the Strategic Air Command (SAC). SAC called Offutt home since November 9, 1948.

The president's plane landed at 2:50 p.m., and the president and key people were herded into what looked like a small brick outhouse. That unassuming doorway leads down into STRATCOM's underground Command Center. The underground building would likely remind an uninitiated visitor (in the unlikely event that someone could ever visit who has not been fully indoctrinated) of a scene out of *War Games*. After being updated by STRATCOM staff, the president teleconferenced with the Pentagon and all of the national intelligence agencies.

No public record of the meeting between the president and his advisors on that day has yet been disclosed. History may eventually tell your grandchildren of the discussion. For now, one can only guess at what the president may have said. It might have sounded a great deal like Slim Pickens did in *Dr. Strangelove*:

"Well, boys, I reckon this is it . . . Now look, boys, I ain't much of a hand at makin' speeches, but I got a pretty fair idea that something doggone important is goin' on back there. And I got a fair idea the kinda personal emotions that some of you fellas may be thinkin'. Heck, I reckon you wouldn't even be human bein's if you didn't have some pretty strong personal feelin's about nuclear combat. I want you to remember one thing, the folks back home is a-countin' on you and by golly, we ain't about to let 'em down. I tell you something else, if this thing turns out to be half as important as I figure it just might be, I'd say that you're all in line for some important promotions and personal citations when this thing's over with. That goes for ever' last one of you regardless of your race, color, or your creed. Now let's get this thing on the hump—we got some flyin' to do."

After about ninety minutes, the president flew back to the White House, leaving the security and serenity of Nebraska behind him, where it remains to this day, at the ready for the next call of duty.

Conspiracy Theory

Conspiracy theorists point to the fact that the Oracle of Omaha and world's richest person, Warren Buffett, was participating in the last of a series of annual golf charity events at Offutt on September 11. Those who love finding connections among newspaper articles and Internet research claim the charity event was planned on that day and location to provide an excuse for a select group of well-to-do who would have normally been in their offices at the World Trade Center. By scheduling a trip to Omaha to give away money and play golf, they avoided dying in the cataclysmic events of the day. Of course—clever planners—this would have been devised about one decade prior, as the the charity tournament was created eight years prior to 2001.

Gee, no wonder these guys are rich. They can really carry out a plan.

Stark Weather, Cold Blood

Bennet

No one cried for the troubled boy gone bad when he was executed in 1959. The series of eleven murders that nineteen-year-old trash collector Charlie Starkweather committed with his fourteen-year-old

Old Sparky jolted Charlie.

girlfriend, Caril Ann Fugate, over two months from December 1, 1957, to January 29, 1958, was horrific and stunningly unusual for the time. The horror included slaying both Fugate's parents and her two-year-old sister, then stuffing them into the outhouse and staying in the house for a few days by deflecting visitors with a sign saying the family had the flu.

It was north of Bennet where a high school couple stopped to see if they could help Charlie with his car troubles. They were murdered for their attempt to help and found in a heap at the bottom of some storm cellar steps.

There was much in this story to capture the nation's attention. Starkweather modeled his look after James Dean's character in *Rebel Without a Cause*, Jim Stark. Parents are a worried lot to begin with, and the thought of a leather-jacketed juvenile delinquent luring a young girl into murdering her family followed by a countryside killing spree only heightened their fears. When Starkweather killed a successful local businessman, the governor called up the National Guard to help with the search.

The media stories influenced a ten-year-old Stephen King, who professed to keeping a scrapbook that included articles about the spree. King once credited Starkweather's influence in an interview by saying, "The very first time I saw a picture of him, I knew I was looking at the future. His eyes were a double zero. There was just nothing there. He was like an outrider of what America might become."

Starkweather influenced many popular culture pieces ranging from Woody Allen's *Take the Money and Run* (1969) to Terence Malick's *Badlands* (1973). Other directors who have references to Starkweather in their work include Steven Spielberg, David Lynch, Oliver Stone, and Peter Jackson. Musical references include Bruce Springsteen's album, *Nebraska*, which Springsteen purportedly considered calling *Starkweather*. Given the fact that many people hear the music but not the lyrics, Nebraska tourism probably benefited from that decision.

"Old Sparky"

Nebraska executed Charlie Starkweather on June 29, 1959. It would be thirty-five years before Nebraska would carry out another execution. Nebraska executed two more before the end of the century. In 2001 the Alabama Supreme Court ruled that electrocution is an unconstitutionally cruel and unusual punishment, thus making Nebraska the only state in the nation using the electric chair as the sole method of execution.

In 2008 Nebraska's unique status changed when the state supreme court decided that the electric chair was an unconstitutional way to administer capital punishment.

With that decision, Nebraska moved from being the last state in the country to use an electric chair for executions to one that no longer has an allowable method of execution in place. The state has not yet passed a law describing what method of capital punishment should replace the chair, which first went into service in 1913.

After he was captured, Starkweather told the bevy of reporters clamoring to know why he did it, "We were only trying to get out of town."

A Podunk Town
Brock

Brock changed its name from Podunk several years ago. The reasons for the change are lost to time. It might have been due to the munificence of a local named Brock, or to honor a local athlete, or simply because the mayor's wife named their son Roscoe instead of his choice, Brock—so the mayor named what he could.

Podunk. The quintessential synonym for Hicktown, USA. Many states once had a town of this name. It may be that the town fathers wanted to avoid duplication; if so, they failed, as more Brocks exist in the United States than do Podunks. And if that was their reason, they could have tried something a bit more original like these other Nebraska towns: Wahoo, Winnetoon, or Worms.

Grip It. Grip It Good.
DeWitt

It's not a tool known for its elegance, but for its ability to do the job when everything else fails. Craftsmen won't turn to it first, but rest assured they have one in their shop, available for emergencies. Unless, of course, they left it clamped onto the underbelly of their old pickup when they put it there to temporarily stop the rattle made by a few too many bolts falling out from an exhaust pipe clamp. Or maybe it's in use as the PRNDL lever (you know—the gear shift), and their teen-age boy has the truck out on a date.

Most every do-it-yourselfer knows that every job is an excuse to buy a new tool. It's important to have the right tool for the job in order to earn that praise from the wife when done:

"Look what I did, honey. I modified that old washing machine we were gonna throw out into a quick-cooling device for a beer keg. Just put the keg in the tub, then fill with ice and turn on spin cycle, and in ten minutes we've got ice-cold beers!"

"Uh-huh. That's nice," is the time-honored reply.

But if lack of time or money prevents that trip to the hardware store to get the newest right tool for the job, the Vise-Grip is the next best thing. It's most often used after the poorly adjusted crescent wrench has made it impossible to turn a hex head on a bolt. By clamping on the Vise-Grip and applying a good deal of personal sweat and private curses, one can completely round off the bolt head to a chewed-up mass of shiny metal.

★ ★

Welders like to use the Vise-Grip to hold pieces being welded and to demonstrate basic thermodynamics—"If you heat something, it gets hot." Many welders can show you the burn scar where they took off their glove to release the Vise-Grip that was connected to the metal they were welding, forgetting all about the fact that heat travels from metal to metal.

But the very best use of the Vise-Grip may be to hold something precisely where you put it. It's not like an extra pair of human hands, which tend to be connected to a voice offering advice or asking how long the job will last. A silent helper is a beautiful thing.

The Vise-Grips were invented here in DeWitt in 1915 by Danish immigrant Bill Petersen and manufactured here from 1924 until 2008.

Bill Goes Wild

Endicott

Imagine a time when the popular culture was full of characters whose exploits were told and retold to the public in ways that glamorized their stories to the point where reality was overcome by myth. You know, a time very much like today, only without TV or radio or movies. Let's just say 1861.

James Butler Hickok, known by those familiar with Wild West legends as Wild Bill, started his wildness in Nebraska on July 12 of that year. At least inasmuch as wildness is measured by gunplay.

Due to his prominent proboscis and an overbite, James Butler was known as "Duck Bill" when he arrived at the Rock Creek Station to work as a freight driver. He was there when the original owners of the station land came to collect payment they hadn't received. Dialogue moved from words to bullets, and by the end of the discussion Hickok had killed three men.

A trial ruled that "Duck Bill" acted in self-defense. A few years later, in 1867, the *Harper's New Monthly Magazine* ran an article written by Colonel George Ward Nichols called "Wild Bill." It seems he decided that "Duck Bill" wasn't as suitable a name for James as "Wild Bill." Hickok grew a moustache to help camouflage his beakiness and lived up to the new name by killing people across the west as he traveled.

The author of the "Wild Bill" article was so derided by local newspapers for the inaccuracies in his story that he moved back east and focused on writing about music. Maybe there's a lesson here for *Entertainment Tonight* and E!?

And It Stoned Me

The Filley Stone Barn lies a couple of miles southwest of Filley. It was built in 1874 by Elijah Filley. Mr. Filley was sick and tired of grasshoppers eating everything in their path—both harvest and storage facilities alike.

Grasshopper cycles were dreadful plagues on the plains in those days. Even today a stand of corn can look as though it was hit by a hailstorm after grasshoppers go through. But nothing can beat the story of so many grasshoppers on the tracks that a train couldn't get enough traction to climb a mild incline.

The barn has been described as the largest known limestone barn in the state.

Just try noshing on this, you bugs.

★ ★

Hot Dog!

Fairbury

Nothing excites members of a Saturday afternoon football crowd like being shot at with a hot dog bazooka. That, and maybe repeated viewings of a wardrobe malfunction.

Every state has its own favorite foods. Nebraskans are fond of the Runza (a dough pocket stuffed with burger and seasoning, also called a "pirogi"), and Dorothy Lynch dressing. But Fairbury is home to the Fairbury hot dogs sold on game days around this part of the state. They are redder than any other dog you've seen, and a bit longer than the bun. What makes them special is the pneumatic gun delivery from the sidelines into the crowd fifty to eighty rows up.

Sure, you've seen these guns elsewhere. But Fairbury's Weiner Schlinger slings wieners into the crowd like no other. Other parts of the state brag that their wurst is the best, but none can hold a candle to the caliber of presentation offered by the Fairbury frank. Be sure to send your package of favorite meats from the Fairbury Steak Company—the big red weiner coupled with Rocky Mountain oysters. Perpetuate the Nebraskan priapic mythology.

Dig It

Fairbury

Many Nebraskans amuse themselves with a spare-time activity that fits the stereotype of the flyover, blue-collar monoculture, such as square dancing and canning jams. But every so often a person with a slightly altered idea of hobby time comes around.

Take the case of Nelson McDowell. In 1915 he took a chisel and a hammer and started to chisel into the face of a sandstone hill. Some folks might have inscribed their name or sculpted an image, but Nelson decided to dig. And dig he did. For at least a decade he carved into this rock overlooking Rose Creek.

He described his hobby as a way to keep himself active and plan for the future, suggesting that this would be a mausoleum for him.

Soft Time

Is it any wonder that this town bears the name "Friend"? Or that its welcome sign says THE WORLD'S BEST FRIEND? It claims to have the smallest police station in the nation. In truth, the other towns making the smallest police station claim point to a phone booth; for the Nebraska version of that joke, you need to travel to Wahoo. When this building was renovated in the '60s, it lost its original tool-shed image and created extra space so that the Nebraska State Patrol could share the facility. That makes it the nation's smallest combined law enforcement office.

It was so much easier to stake the claim as smallest in the nation in days gone by, when Ripley's Believe It or Not would make the claim for you. Which it did once.

Bigger isn't necessarily better for the local constabulary.

When he died in 1937 at the age of eighty, the interior of the mausoleum contained a heavily graffitied anteroom and an interior, circular
room with a domed ceiling and two 6-foot carved slabs that would be
a suitable resting spot.

A Nebraska state law prevents interment on private property; Nelson McDowell is buried at the Fairbury Cemetery. Rules, rules. Nor
was the bid to put the mausoleum on the National Register of Historic
Places accepted. More rules. The state of Nebraska did accept the
land for use as a public park, and the rules of the state discourage
the time-honored practice of carving names in the rock. No matter—
there are plenty of inscriptions in the rock, including place names like
"Devil's Slide" and "Pulpit Rock." The sign above the 6-foot carved
entryway was done professionally by a local monument artisan hired
by McDowell.

McDowell's Tomb isn't easy to find. An unmarked trail winds away
from a dead-end road that looks as though it is a favorite drinking
haunt for local youth.

Directions from Jefferson County tourism folks: "Begin at Fairbury
City Park and drive south on Frederick Street. Follow a curve onto
Crystal Springs Road and again onto 566 Avenue. Continue moving
south on 566 Avenue until you reach a dead end (about 2 miles south
on NE 8). The Wildlife Management parking area is on the right-hand
side of the road. Over the railroad tracks and across the bridge, follow the south bank of Rose Creek and in less than half a mile you will
reach the Mausoleum."

Andy the Footless Goose
Harvard

Fifteen minutes of fame came to Gene Fleming by way of an act of
kindness to a gosling born at his sister-in-law's farm near Harvard.
Fleming noticed the gray goose while on a family visit. Andy hatched
without feet about two years prior to the visit, and had managed
to move around in a stumpy sort of webless walk. Fleming said his

★ ★

ANDY
THE
GOOSE
1987–1991

"ANDY" THE FOOTLESS GOOSE, BORN WITHOUT WEBS AND
TOES, UNABLE TO WALK AND SWIM PROPERLY WAS PUT ON
THE ROAD AGAIN BY HIS MASTER WHO INSTALLED SIZE "0"
BABY SHOES ON "ANDY" AND THEN TAUGHT HIM TO WALK.
ANDY" WAS AN INSPIRATION TO THOUSANDS OF
HANDICAPPED CHILDREN ACROSS THE U.S.A. AND
FOREIGN COUNTRIES TO TRY A LITTLE HARDER AND
DON'T GIVE UP, MAKE ANOTHER TRY.
"ANDY" WAS IN READERS DIGEST, PEOPLE MAGAZINE
AND MANY OTHERS. "ANDY" WAS ALSO ON THE JOHNNY
CARSON TELEVISION SHOW.

MEMORIAL DONATED BY PALMER BROTHERS GRANITE CO.
HOLDREGE, NEBRASKA

"Please, Louise. Get me offa my knees."

affiliation with the local Shriners, a philanthropic group serving crippled children, guided his actions after meeting Andy.

He gave his sister-in-law a pair of geese to replace Andy and Andy's mate, Polly. Then he took the two to his acreage near Hastings. Fleming spent several hours training Andy how to walk with a pair of modified infant's patent leather shoes, and when Andy caught on, he became a terror on two feet. Andy was soon running and swimming with the rest. The leather shoes only lasted a month, so Fleming fashioned a pair of Nikes that proved more durable.

Andy the Footless Goose gained fame as a can-do gander who overcame diversity with the help of his cobbler. *People Magazine* ran a January 30, 1989, article, and a few days later fellow Nebraskan Johnny Carson invited Andy and Fleming to the February 1, 1989, airing of *The Tonight Show*, where Andy demonstrated his walking and swimming prowess for the nation. People were either amused at the novel relationship between bird and benefactor or found inspiration in the gander's game sense of endurance.

Those were heady days for the Andy the Footless Goose, who made countless appearances at schools and other local groups. But it all came to a horrific and twisted end in October 1991, when Andy was found in a City of Hastings park, decapitated, mutilated, but with his Texas-made cowboy boots still on.

Local citizens and national fans alike were outraged and raised $10,000 as reward money. The culprit was never caught, and the money is still in the bank. Poor Gene Fleming buried his friend in his yard outside of Hastings.

A monument company in nearby Holdrege donated a black granite monument to commemorate the memory of Andy. It's at the Fleming farm outside of Hastings, 4389 East Hadco Road.

Swing Time
Hebron

If it's possible to capture both the positive and negative aspects of a stereotype with one image, it's possible with Hebron's porch swing. Do you recall, from among the countless movie and television porch swing scenes, the one in the movie *To Kill a Mockingbird*? It was there that Atticus read to Scout, it was there that Atticus overheard his children talking about vague memories of their mother, and it was there that Scout took Boo after he emerged from the shadows. In this movie and in so many other stories, the porch swing offers an iconic image of family, home, and love.

And with that same image, marketing mavens on Madison Avenue imply a hick-sterism or bumpkin-ess found only here in Flyover Country.

Swing both ways. www.NebraskaTheGoodLife.com

So how should a small town use the porch swing image to demonstrate both Heartland values and sophistication equal to porch swing owners looking out from Martha's Vineyard? Why, the answer is as obvious as your favorite piece of Americana: take it and make it bigger. Not just bigger, but biggest.

That's just what the good folks in Hebron have done. They've turned some extra pieces of center pivot irrigation pipe into a 32-foot-long swing that can seat from sixteen to twenty adults, depending on their ability to fit into shrinking airplane and stadium seats. It's the biggest non-porch-perched porch swing in the world.

Not that the record keepers over at the Guinness Book of World Records will agree. Nor do they disagree. It turns out that it costs potential record holders some hard cash to create a new category. And since the swing was built with a cash budget of $250, along

★ ★

with volunteer contributions of time and materials, folks in Hebron decided their marketing would be word-of-mouth.

It sits under the shade of several trees in downtown Hebron, complete with a squeak.

Seating is currently available in Roosevelt Park at Fifth and Jefferson Streets.

Boys Don't Cry
Humboldt

The Hollywood treatment of a Nebraska crime also earned national acclaim for a Nebraska native as an actress. While star Hilary Swank tends to refer to Bellingham, Washington, as the town of her youth, she was indeed born in Lincoln, Nebraska. But just try to get her to admit it in an interview. It seems as though she is as thrilled with her Nebraska connection as Nebraskans are with the fact that an attention-getting Best Actress Academy Award came with this particular story about Nebraska.

The story is about the girl born Teena Brandon, who identified herself as a male named Brandon Teena. (*Nomen est omen* was the Roman phrase, which translates as "names are destiny." One wonders whether a cautionary note for parents about naming children with two first names is in order. Certainly several fictional heroes have done well—Clark Kent, Bruce Wayne, James Kirk, and most recently Ricky Bobby. But so have actual people such as Henry James and Jon Stewart. And Nebraska-born actress Sandy Dennis puts to rest any claim related to gender differences between the two names as a behavioral cause. Never mind.)

Teena was the victim of a hate crime, beaten and raped on Christmas Eve by two local men who had discovered her gender. Teena went to the local sheriff and filed charges but was met with bigotry and indifference. The Nebraska Supreme Court later referred to the local actions as "beyond all possible bounds of decency."

Tragically, the indifference seemed to give license to the two men, who murdered Teena and two others on New Year's Eve in 1993.

23 mph

Long before Hollywood made a movie about the number 23, Lake Waconda residents had an affinity for the number.

As any numerologist worth his salt can tell you, 23 is a number of significance. All of history's important events are tied to the number in some regard. From the days when Caesar died from twenty-three stab wounds to the tragedy of September 11, 2001 (some artful adding of the date, 09-11-2001, i.e., 9 + 11 and 2 + 1 = 23), all events can be tied to 23.

All one needs to understand these connections are a calculator and an ability to make leaps of logic that less imaginative minds simply cannot grasp.

So how is it that this small lakeside community decided to set the speed limit at 23 mph? Was the Ouija board consulted? Tea leaves? A grant from Dr Pepper to promote the twenty-three flavors blended in their drink? Nope. The guy who placed the order at the sign shop said that 25 mph was boring—every other town has one of those. The guy taking the order said not to use an even number. And there you have it.

Does it matter? Not really. The local constabulary uses enforcement discretion and won't stop anyone until they go over 25 mph.

It was the release of the independent film *Boys Don't Cry* in 1999 shortly after the hate crime murder of a gay man in Wyoming that helped propel the film into public view. CNN ran a story in 2003, crediting the telling and timing of the story with activating the

★ ★

transgender and gay communities into action, demanding the enact-
ment of new hate crime legislation.

It's a story of how individual role play led to local foul play and
eventually to national rule changes. You can never predict from
whence change comes.

Name the baby what you like.

America's Number 2 Loo
Louisville

In a state that takes competition seriously, and in the streak-breaking
year for the flagship competitive team, the Nebraska Cornhuskers,
joy and pride still found its way to Louisville. It was there that the Art
Chicks Gallery, a small eatery and "girlfriends gallery," earned national
honors as the second best restroom in the United States for 2004.

While many local University of Nebraska football fans found themselves hoping for a bid to even a low-level postseason spot at a deri-
sively described "Toilet Bowl," it turns out it was a literal toilet bowl
that kept Nebraska in the national limelight. How nice that in a state
where do-it-yourself decorators have showcased the height of their
talents in multiple home, bar, and diner restrooms with Cornhusker
football themes, someone brought diversity and flair to powder room
paraphernalia.

A word or two of advice to would-be visitors of this Nebraska
attraction:

The restroom has been redesigned. It's gone undersea. Part of this
was due to a shift in management, part from a distaste for same-
ness, even with a design that most locals would call unique. How nice
not to be bound up in the past; after all, doing that would move the
bathroom back outdoors into its own building, stocked with corncobs
and catalogs. We appreciate those who do not dwell too long on the
laurels of previous success— especially in a bathroom.

Male visitors to this attraction need to exercise caution. This cafe
caters to women. When I stopped in, it appeared to me that the

No reading material needed—a feast for the eyes.

clientele were mostly inebriated women—perhaps not intoxicated by alcohol but by the atmosphere of overwhelming estrogen. I was (pleasantly) surprised to be on the receiving end of wolf whistles and catcalls as I walked through on my way to the restroom. But other men may not be as comfortable with all the attention. Watch your back—they will.

Art Chicks—A Girlfriends Gallery is located at 127 Main Street. It's open on Friday and Saturday for lunch seatings at 11:30 a.m. and

★ ★

1:00 p.m. Reservations are recommended; the minimum age is sixteen. For more information, call (402) 234-2669 or go to www .nebrartchicks.com.

World's Biggest Rut
Milford exit 382

Just as cross-continent travel changed in nature from the distinctly American journeys of family Joad to family Griswald, so too changed the face of roadside vendors. At the end of a day, travelers once found camps near a stream or meadow, which later gave way to entrepreneurs who built gas stations and campgrounds to give travelers more time and bigger audiences for swapping stories of awful

Just who are you calling a Westward Ho?

weather and crazy drivers. In time the competition among roadside vendors sparked a creative drive to gain attention from drivers or their bored but vocal passengers. Bigger signs, free ice water, and various marketing come-ons were used. How better to encourage a stop than with unusual roadside architecture, sometimes referred to as vernacular architecture.

The heyday of this specialized design and construction was decades ago in California; perhaps designing donut-shaped donut shops or ice-cream-cone-shaped ice-cream stands offered theater designers (or wannabes) some additional cash or design portfolio credibility. During that time, wigwam-shaped souvenir stands beckoned car-seat cowboys off the road as families rode westward. In the early 1970s one landowner built his own version of a western outpost on the north side of I-80 at exit 382.

If what is left is any indication, the Westward Ho Park had its day as a photo opportunity campground and gift shop for the road-weary traveler. But today one sees only the outer shell of an oversize (50 feet tall, 30 feet wide, and 50 feet long) covered wagon, where one could once fuel up the station wagon and peer across the road at several oversize wooden tepees.

It's still worth a picture as the World's Largest Covered Wagon. But since it hasn't moved in a while, the largest wagon rut is gone.

No Crop Circles or Craft Fairs Here
Marquette

Nebraska is surprising in its subtle wealth of natural variety. The same is true for its cultural offerings. You can be driving through miles upon miles of bovine personality and agricultural monoculture when—*whammo!*—you're suddenly face-to-face with a mind-bending experience like Art Farm. For more than twenty-five years, Art Farm has tilled creative soil in the pastoral quietude of a remote central Nebraska farmstead.

★ ★

Spread across a rolling prairie landscape near the Platte River north of Aurora, Art Farm offers a month or two of peace and quiet far from the madding crowd for a handful of professional artists from around the world. Residencies include living accommodations, a private studio, and a fearful amount of heavy equipment for most any type of artistic endeavor, as well as technical support from staff and daily assistance from Art Farm interns. In exchange, visiting artists are asked to contribute twelve hours of weekly elbow grease to maintain the facilities.

Art Farm is well off the beaten path, 80 miles west of Lincoln and about 15 miles north of I-80. The owners caution that if you can't get to sleep without the melody of police sirens or your spirit craves the occasional exuberance of a bar fight, this may not be the ideal experience for you. This place is about concentrated introspection, and the only rowdies are crickets and horseflies. Excitement is pretty much limited to watching native prairie grasses repopulate the plains.

At the center of Art Farm is a cluster of four old relocated barns connected into a single 12,000-square-foot complex. These buildings were saved from the ravages of everything from locusts to lightning and have found new life as studio areas for the visiting artists. Residents stay nearby in a 100-year-old farmhouse.

The first of the barn buildings was moved to the Art Farm campus in 1975, and the nonprofit was formed in 1993. Visitors can roam through twenty acres of "sculpture prairie," where artists have installed large-scale creations of all kinds. It's best to call ahead before you visit, or you can attend one of the occasional events between May and November (check their Web site). The premier annual public gathering is the Art Harvest on Halloween weekend. It's the best time to hobnob and explore this unique contribution to the world of art a long, long way from the nearest diva or dilettante.

Art Farm is located at 1306 West 21 Road. For more information, call (402) 854-3120 or go to www.artfarmnebraska.org.

Grave Sights: Dead Wood

Nebraska City

Be certain that you will suffer the verbal jabs from your friends, family, and neighbors if they find out about your visit to this unusual cemetery ("You went where?" "You did what?"), but be just as certain that you will want to take a picture when you stop here.

The Wyuka Cemetery is, er, populated with a relatively large number of unusual granite or limestone sculptures that serve as headstones or family plot markers. Most of the unusual ones here look like tree stumps—varying in height from ground level to 20 feet or more. One might guess that Nebraska City's well-known identity as a Tree City shapes local community action with a bandwagon hyperdrive, starting with children planting samplings and dressing up as trees in an Arbor

Writing this isn't as easy as it looks.

Arbor Day— That's the Thicket!

When you drive through the thicketed hills of Nebraska City, a little burg overlooking the Missouri River in eastern Nebraska it's hard to imagine that one of the early settlers once bemoaned the lack of trees. The abundance of trees here is due in large measure to one citizen, J. Sterling Morton, who did everything he could to popularize the practice of planting trees to change the landscape.

Morton was the editor of the state's first newspaper and an amateur silviculturist. Using his print forum and position as a civic leader, he proposed and advocated for an Arbor Day in 1872. Incentives provided by the endorsement of the state Agricultural Board combined with effective press helped lead to an incredible million-tree planting on the first Arbor Day. Arbor Day became an official state holiday two years later. Since then, all fifty states and at least thirty countries have adopted their own version of the holiday.

Tree planting was a practice that served Nebraska well—even leading the legislature to adopt the Tree Planter State as its official nickname in 1895. Nebraska kept this as the official state name until 1945, when popular sentiment swung from planting trees to husking corn.

Planting trees is a good way to sequester carbon. R. Neibel

Day play, then moving to workplace fund drives and corporate community sponsorships of Arbor Day parade floats. It's easy to imagine citizens so thoroughly imprinted with the timber traditions that local funerary traditions transformed to include a treestone as a permanent marker. Indeed, Arbor Day founder J. Sterling Morton's family plot arguably has the largest treestone monument to be found anywhere.

Perhaps it was the practice of the Omaha-based insurance company Woodmen of the World to pay for a tree-themed inscription for its clients, with a high level of participation in Nebraska City. Or maybe it was a Victorian penchant for rustic images that also found its way into the Sears catalog at the time. Or maybe the local headstone artisan's nickname was Woody.

Whatever the reason, when people in Tree City were planted in their graves in Wyuka Cemetery, many chose to use a headstone in the shape of a tree. But not all. Be sure to stop near the entrance of the cemetery to look at the family plot that has a full-size roll-top desk as a family marker.

Funny Faces

Nelson

Picture a small town in Nebraska—easy to do, most towns in Nebraska are small. As you look down the bricked main street and most likely the highway through town, what do you see? Maybe you see an Edward Hopper–esque coffee shop serving Norman Rockwell fare just down the street from the Andrew Carnegie–funded library. A dog crosses the street at the same time each day, checking out the scraps in the alleyway out back. There's a bar, a beautician, and a few storefronts gone empty when the big-box stores opened up forty-five minutes away. The grain elevator is down on the edge of town at the railroad crossing; it's there where you can pick up a feed cap during the day while at night you can watch meth addicts trying to steal anhydrous ammonia without getting frostbit or arrested.

★ ★

Every small town in Nebraska shares at least part of this iconography. It's a ready framework that helps to define the local culture. Imagine the reaction when a local businessman decided to do something just a little bit different. That's what William Stansbury did over a century ago, and locals still don't know what to make of it.

Stansbury, so frugal that locals described him as "tight as bark on a birch tree," decided to add totally unnecessary and completely endearing sculptures to his building back in 1899. Twelve stone heads and two small owls peer out of the side of the Stansbury building at slightly higher than eye level. Some of the sculptures are of national figures of the time, such as President Theodore Roosevelt, Spanish American War hero Admiral Dewey, frontiersman and Calmity Jane's foster father Parson Bob, Buffalo Bill, and renowned crack marksman

Theodore
Roosevelt

Kissin'
Jack
Adamson

Jack said, "Pucker up, honey, we're goin' for a ride."
Teddy said, "Bully!"

Diamond Dick. Others figures were local personalities such as an auctioneer, undertaker, One-Eye Riley, Indian Joe, and businessman Stansbury.

The stories about the local characters have largely disappeared, but Kissin' Jack Adamson's fame is still known around Nelson. Jack got his nickname by trying to convince all the girls who rode in his hack from the depot into town to give him a kiss. Jack's quirky visage in full pucker on the side of the building gives a whole new meaning to the term *stoneface*.

The Stansbury building is on the southwest corner of Main and Fourth Streets.

Git-R-Done
Palmyra

Popular American cultural icons come and go; Andy Warhol may not have gotten it right when he said we will all have our fifteen minutes of fame, but enough common folk have grown rich and famous that everyone uses their own personal piece of that dream to make it through their otherwise unexamined days.

Dan Whitney, known to many in America as Larry the Cable Guy, and to the youngsters in the crowd as the voice of Mater (rhymes with "tater," the abbreviation of potato—not to be confused with the Latin word for "mother," *mater*) in the animated movie *Cars*, hails from this part of Nebraska. He's unrepentant in his celebration of blue-collar values—a rabid Husker football fan, and now owner or part owner of rodeo bulls and the sale barn here.

Not everyone knows about the culture of the sale barn. While corn, soybeans, or other grains are bought and sold with a phone call to the local grain elevator, a trip to the sale barn is a slightly different trip to the agricultural traditions of America. It's either the busiest or only place in town to get breakfast and lunch on sale days; you can munch on burgers at the counter while watching burgers on the hoof herded in and out of trailers and through chutes outside the window.

★ ★

Up, Up, and Away

The longest documented trip taken by tornado debris was 280 miles, from Great Bend, Kansas, to Palmyra, Nebraska, in November 1915. It was documented when a cancelled check was found among the debris of the tornado just outside of Palmyra—a check swept off somebody's desk in Great Bend.

This provides definite proof for those who want a reality check on the *Wizard of Oz* story—when you get swept up in a Kansas tornado, that dreamscape over the rainbow where you land is really called "Nebraska."

Sale barn transactions are the livestock equivalent of the used car dealer—where the term "horse trader" indicates both great negotiating skills and a reminder to the buyer, "Beware."

Sale barns are rife with stories of contrivances to improve sale prices; there's one of the half-wild horse that was ridden around by the best rodeo-ridin' cowboy prior to the sale until the horse had bucked so much it was plumb tuckered out. By seeming coincidence, that's the time when the sale list had an opening for the auctioneer's skinny eight-year-old daughter to ride it into the arena, looking all the world like the perfect horse for any child. Woe to the purchaser who ends up with a wild horse like that when he gets it home and finds a bucking bronc when he opens the trailer door.

A Low Point
Rulo

Multiple geological features of interest exist in Flyover Country: The highest point in the state out in the panhandle (see that chapter) lies atop the very slightest of rises, the sand hills in the middle of the state have a sandiness cloaked entirely by grass cover, the continent's largest groundwater aquifer recharge area isn't visible to the above-ground traveler, and the toadstool-shaped sandstone formations are all but forgotten in the shadow of the Badlands just to the north. So, okay, there's nothing in Nebraska as noticeable as the Grand Canyon or Mount Rainier; in this part of the state the leastest is the mostest—the lowest point in Nebraska is mired in mud.

If you are for some reason out on a waymarking adventure of national low points (and how do you explain that quest to your friends?), be sure to travel to this one. It's visible from a climb up the bluff about 6 miles south of Rulo, where an 1854 marker known as

You take the low road.

★ ★

the Iron Monument is marked by a highway sign on a pleasant Missouri River–side drive to the Kansas border, the 40th parallel.

Actually getting to the low point is a bit more of an adventure. A levee road runs from the highway out to the river, but it's not a public thoroughfare. You may find it easier to get low by hopping on a floatation device upriver in Rulo and riding the current downward to the border with Kansas and Missouri. When you get to the point where the land gives up its Nebraskan identity to become either Missouri or Kansas, you'll be at the spot where Nebraska is at its lowest.

Do Not Open Until 2025

Seward

Time was when a man who wanted to let future generations know what life was like "when I was a boy" would write a book or annotate the family photo album. Seward resident Harold Davisson decided that he wanted something a bit more tangible for his descendents. So he dug a hole in the front yard of The House of Davisson and built a concrete and steel vault, into which he put an estimated 5,000 items that represented his then sixty-seven-year-old life in 1975.

Could you pull together 5,000 keepsakes from your memories of 1975? Watergate convictions kicked off that year, *The Rocky Horror Picture Show* began on Broadway, and Bill Gates founded Microsoft. Local wags thought Davisson put in items that weren't selling at his hardware store, but at least part of the contributions to the time capsule came from other stores in Seward. Two new vehicles, a Chevy Vega and a blue Kawasaki motorcycle, were put in the original vault along with letters and other memorabilia. Ever ahead of his time as well as present in it, he included a blue leisure suit a full two years before *Saturday Night Fever* was released.

The original time capsule that was sealed on July 4, 1975, measures 20 feet by 8 feet by 6 feet and weighs 45 tons; it captured the honorific as "The World's Largest Time Capsule" from the Guinness Book of Records in 1977. After some purported squabbles with the

This is no middlin' pyramid.

International Time Capsule Society (Who knew? The International Time Capsule Society?), Guinness made the politically expedient if not Solomon-esque decision to drop the category altogether. To maintain bragging rights, Davisson added the pyramid above the original capsule in 1983 and put a well-travelled 1975 Datsun in there along with several items donated by the community.

The plan is to open the time capsule during the Fourth of July festivities in 2025, fifty years after it was sealed. If you want to catch a peek of the pyramid, you can find it, along with some other photoworthy kitsch, at 318 Hillcrest Drive.

Happy Father's Day!
South Bend

If you are incredibly citified, a super-urbane metrosexual, you may have never been introduced to a delicacy found largely in cattle country known as Rocky Mountain oysters. If you learned of them from

Omaha-born George Edward Pandray thought the term "time bomb" a bit too explosive and coined the term "time capsule" to describe part of the Westinghouse exhibit at the 1939 World's Fair.

an older brother, you probably tasted them before finding out their bovine origins. These oysters aren't found in a stream or even on cows. Nope, they were once found on bulls, but because you have them on the end of your fork, those same animals are now steers. Rocky Mountain oysters are in fact steer testicles. Don't accept bull testicles, because they are still attached to the bull, which could offer you an entirely new meaning to the phrase "food frenzy."

Not that they need to come from young bulls; hogs and turkeys are often also the source. The fruits of castration are sometimes called prairie oysters, calf fries, cowboy caviar, or even tendergroins.

Folks around South Bend are familiar with such things, so don't dwell much on idioms developed for sensitive ears or the censorship-in-schools crowd and other polite company—they call their annual feed the Testicle Festival, and what's more, they hold it on Father's Day weekend.

So go a little nuts and take Poppa out for a festive celebration of his day. It's a grand time for outdoor barbecue, live bands, and down-home family fun. Here's a tip to offer the squeamish: If you don't want the deep-fried or sliced and sautéed nads on your plate, ask for some *huevos* instead. Things always taste better when ordered in a foreign tongue.

The festival is just a couple of miles west of South Bend at the Round the Bend Steakhouse and Saloon.

Hog Herdin' Hunks

Unadilla

Do you remember the scene at the beginning of *The Wizard of Oz* (when the movie was still black and white—supposedly done to emphasize the colorless life on the farm) when Dorothy fell into the hog pen, and Hickory or Hunk or Zeke pulled her out of harm's way? (No joke, hogs can clamp down with a fearsome bite—you should remember that when you get out of your car in some parts of eastern Nebraska.) Here in Nebraska live three hog farmers who, had they been in that movie, would have kept that lonely little farm girl down on the farm and made it seem plenty colorful, too.

These three brothers do what many farmers do—work a second job. But rather than clerking at the local lumberyard, when the Bartling brothers work that second job, they do so as models. You may have seen them on the cover of your favorite romance novel.

It may seem like a strange pairing of skills, but if you think about it a bit more, you could soon identify traits common to both occupations, model and hog farmer:

Both models and hog farmers are guaranteed to be the drop-dead, stop-'em-in-their-tracks center of attention of any event they go to from work without stopping to change their clothes.

Both tend to find themselves isolated from the rest of society. That can make their ideas sound good when they talk to each other, but not so much when placed under broader scrutiny. It's a little like being a politician on Capitol Hill.

Some days, it seems that everyone around you is just a piece of meat.

Both agree that *Charlotte's Web* and *Babe* are great entertainment.

Both know that the squeal is the part you don't sell.

Both know the importance of a mud bath for maintaining personal well-being.

★ ★

So when you are in southeast Nebraska and can't find the Bartling brothers, be sure to try their brand of pork product: You'll know it by its Hickory Hunk label, Zeke.

Groundhog King
Unadilla

Bill Murray plays a character in *Groundhog Day* who struggles with reliving a day in his life, over and over again. The day he relives is the day of celebration in Punxsutawney, Pennsylvania, home to the most celebrated groundhog in America, Punxsutawney Phil.

But one thing Nebraskans know is that weather predictions from out east are as unreliable as the weather is in Nebraska. Whatever the reason, Unadilla has broken up late-winter doldrums with their own celebration of Groundhog Day since 1987. Their event uses a stuffed groundhog named Unadilla Bill.

Just before dawn on Groundhog Day, a local official takes Unadilla Bill down from his perch on a beer cooler in The Bar and heads outside to put Bill down in the middle of Main Street. Then the official shadow observation takes place at 7:30 as the sun rises over the stores on the street. It's enough to bring celebrants out of The Bar to watch, prior to a day of festivities, a parade, and beer.

Unadilla Bill enjoys the day, even though one might find emotion difficult to discern in his motionless visage. He has been taped to the top of parade vehicles, run up the Main Street flagpole, and pretty much put in various poses and places one normally wouldn't attempt with a live groundhog. (Have you ever seen the teeth on one of those things? They are definitely built for chucking wood!)

In order to reduce the chance for tomfoolery by Unadilla Bill (or his helpers) during the rest of the year, The Bar uses an electronic leash of sorts to let them know when he moves from his perch on the beer cooler behind the bar.

In 1988 then Lieutenant Governor Bill Nichol proclaimed Unadilla the Groundhog Capital of Nebraska.

★ ★

Greetings from Unadilla Bill

**What's that up on the fridge? It's a stuffed rodent.
Doesn't everyone have one?** Robert Brandt

The Bar is located at 359 Main Street. For more information, call (402) 828-2800.

Aggies in Nebraska
York

Marbles don't hold much meaning in this world of text messaging and video games. If today's youth knows anything of marbles, it's more likely to be tied to a memory from the movie *Hook*, in which one character, Tootles, confesses that he has lost his.

Time was when marbles provided a schoolyard introduction to wagering, gamesmanship, and "friendly" competition that could readily transfer to billiards or office betting pools. Marbles were once found in the pockets of most kids because they were part of many childhood games, be it multiple variations of schoolyard games honing eye-hand coordination or board games of strategy such as Chinese checkers. These games introduced kids to the different types of marbles, such as cat's-eyes, alleys, aggies, pureys, clearies, or steelies. It seems that many of the descriptive terms used in marble games rhymed with a dwarf named Sneezy.

Lee's Legendary Marble Museum is the public display of Lee Batterton's once-private collection of marbles. Lee turned sixty-eight in 2001, the year he opened his museum. His collection offers an impressive variety of marbles from around the world and offers the casual student and professional alike an opportunity to grow their knowledge about the history and craft of marble making. Numerous collector's items are on display in several wall cases. Special lighting is reserved for the marbles that contain uranium—the black light creates a 1960s sci-fi iridescent glow so intense you can almost hear the Moog synthesizer cuing up in the background.

Every year the museum hosts a meeting of the Great Plains Marble Society, where marble cognoscenti gather to swap stories and compare collections. On most days, however, you can learn more than you ever thought was possible to know about marbles from Batterton's sister-in-law, who manages the collection and store. She's modest about her marble knowledge but is on the ball and a straight shooter who will help any visitor polish up their marble know-how.

The museum is located at 3120 South Lincoln Avenue, north of I-80 about 1 mile.

4

South Central

"**B**ottomlands" may not sound like a particularly appealing part of the state, but that's because you're hung up on the "bottom" part. "Swamp land" doesn't exactly inspire a tourism boom either, but both are highly productive ecosystems and interesting places to visit. The southwestern stretches of Nebraska feature some

Greetings from
the Flat Earth Society

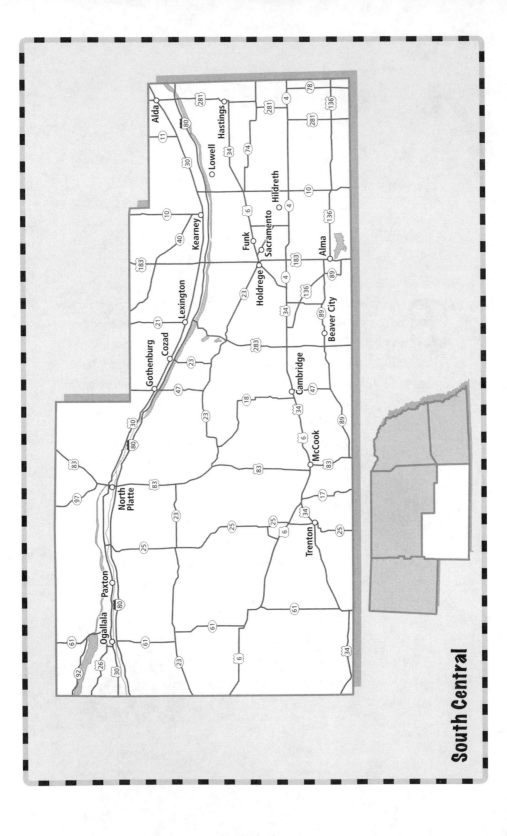

South Central

✦ ✦

of the finest wildlife viewing, boating, fishing, and endless driving in the entire state. In fact, on a mile-for-mile basis, I-80 doesn't get any longer than this. Blame it on the Platte River, which trudges nearly the entire length of the state. "Platte" means "flat," and they weren't kidding when they named this river. It's so flat and wide that it inspired a favorite Nebraska insult—"His mind is like the Platte: a mile wide and an inch deep."

But you don't have to look very far to find unique attractions here. More than half a million sandhill cranes create a spectacle as they make their annual spring migration through an area between Grand Island and Kearney. It is among the most impressive natural wonders of Nebraska, and tourists flock to the area to witness fields packed with the redheaded birds.

The region is dotted with reservoirs built to control another prominent river in the region, the Republican, which parallels the Kansas border and feeds some of the most productive farmland in the state. Southwest Nebraska has a strong sense of its place in American history, too, which includes the Oregon, Mormon, and Pony Express Trails, which witnessed hundreds of thousands of early pioneers crossing the continent in search of gold and new ground.

And don't you worry—there are plenty of oddball attractions to satisfy the meandering mind. From imaginatively monikered towns like Beaver City, Mascot, Assumption, Republican City, and Hamlet to the curious capital of the region—Harold Warp's Pioneer Village—you won't be disappointed that you veered off the main drag. Who would want to miss out on an area that played host to thousands of prisoners of war during World War II and also hosts the only Frank Lloyd Wright home in the whole darn state? Come on, you're up for it, so come on down to the Bottomlands. They're not what you think unless you've completely bottomed out on the chapter title. In which case, too bad for you.

★ ★

How Do You Tell the Difference Between a Husker Fan and a Sandhill Crane?
Alda

As a species, Nebraskans tend to gather in large groups at certain times of the year. In autumn they wear red clothing and crowd together—80,000 strong—in Memorial Stadium at the University of Nebraska-Lincoln to hoot and holler and proclaim their loyalty in a ritual that goes back to the late nineteenth century. These are the Husker faithful, and Nebraskans are proud to tell you that Memorial Stadium is the third-largest community in the state on game days.

Much larger numbers of red-capped critters gather along the Platte River in the spring to hoot and holler and proclaim their loyalty in a ritual dating back about nine million years. (Or 6,000 years, if you're up to a visit from the Kansas State School Board.) These are the sandhill cranes, whose annual stopover along an 80-mile stretch of the Platte River roughly between Grand Island and Kearney creates a spectacle that sends bird lovers into swoons of ecstasy.

Husker fans generally linger at Memorial Stadium for several hours. They are overfed to begin with, but that doesn't stop them from consuming large quantities of oversize pretzels, hot dogs, popcorn, and soft drinks. Sandhill cranes spend around a month feeding in cornfields near the river. They can add 15 percent to their body weight in anticipation of the long migration north to Canada or Alaska.

Husker fans participate in a variety of social dances during the typical football game. The most complex of these is known as "The Wave" and consists of everyone in a section rising to their feet, hands in the air, and sitting down again in quick succession, proceeding from section to section and progressing around the stadium. This creates the appearance of a wave rushing through the stands.

Sandhill cranes engage in a social dance consisting of repeated jumping, bobbing, and bowing motions with wings outstretched. It looks either graceful or silly, depending on your perspective, and it is either a courting gesture or a general expression of approval at having

⋆ ⋆

It's easy to see the difference. Even though they spend all their time among the residual corn husks, this group doesn't wear enough red to be mistaken as part of Husker Nation. www.RickRasmussen.com

a good time hanging out along the river with unlimited free food (leftover corn kernels) at their disposal.

Husker fans make loud noises whenever the team scores a touchdown or when officials make a particularly egregious penalty call.

Sandhill cranes have a distinctive set of calls to warn others away or to keep in touch with family members. The bugling duet call establishes a pair of cranes as a couple and warns others not to interfere with this social arrangement.

Husker games are preceded and followed by a traffic jam extending most of the distance between Lincoln and Omaha. Traffic

★ ★

congestion associated with sandhill cranes seems to occur mostly on the ground in the most desirable feeding spots. Once airborne, the cranes seem to have a pretty good system for merging, passing, and exceeding posted speed limits with a minimum of midair collisions and subsequent insurance claims.

Memorial Stadium is the first thing you see upon entering Lincoln from the downtown exit off I-80. Sandhill crane viewing is best begun with a visit to the Wings Over the Platte Visitors Center at the Alda exit (exit 305) on I-80.

Pie Me a River
Alma

Nature's a wonderful thing. Except that it's so darn . . . natural. Just as humans tend to congregate in cities, birds tend to flock, fish like to school, and bison move in herds. There was a time when bison were too numerous to count unless one was willing to sit and wait for several hours while a thundering herd of a million or so moved past.

As the bison moved, they grazed and drank from nearby river waters. And as happens when animals eat, they excrete. It's only natural. So with a million of the continent's largest mammals eating and all, it wasn't hard to tell where they had been. It would be hard to miss the telltale droppings. That's why one of the polite translations of the Pawnee names for the Republican River was Manure River.

It makes sense. The town name for Anaktuvuk Pass near the Gates of the Arctic Park in Alaska is often explained as "the place where the caribou poop," because the pass provides a commonly used trail for the local and still large caribou herds.

But while Anaktuvuk retains its colorful name, someone decided that Manure River ought to be renamed the Republican River, which is how it's now labeled on Nebraska maps. It would be darn silly for anyone to suggest any connection whatsoever between the former name and the current one. As the song says, "you can't roller-skate in a buffalo herd," and you ought not try connecting the two names in this

First Impressions: The Long and the Flat of It

Nebraska is known for many things (okay, two things: corn and football), but most people who visit the state have a single enduring memory. It is the 500-mile straight line out of here known as I-80. Millions of long-haul truckers and families headed for a Colorado vacation fondly recall the unique sensation they get while crossing Nebraska. It's the feeling that for ten brief hours there is no curvature to the earth's surface. In fact, the name "Nebraska" comes from an Otoe Indian word meaning, "flatter than a Kansas pool table."

Actually the word *Nebraska* comes from a Native American term meaning "flat water." And the French word for *flat* was used to name the Platte River, along which I-80 travels. So when you're driving across Nebraska (meaning "flat") along the Platte (meaning "flat") River, you can relax. The only thing between you and the border is 100,000 eighteen-wheelers.

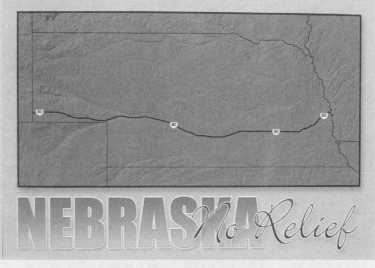

You just can't find any relief in Nebraska. Authors/Dan Griggs Images

very Republican district of a very Republican state. Besides, politicians have a hard enough time keeping their names out of the mud as it is.

Night Owl, Day Hawk
Cambridge

The Lime Creek Observatory is unique for this part of the country.

Many locals spend evenings gazing at their navel or switching channels to find current Husker games or new statistics and gossip so they might continue the chronic daytime discussions about how their personal fanaticism about college athletics compares to fanatics of collegiate athletes in other parts of the United States. But a curious few live in the state who spend their time after sunset analyzing the relationships between all things extraterrestrial. There is one among these few who has had more success than the rest; his name is Robert Lindholm.

Lindholm has used his retirement well by spending hours scouring the heavens to find "minor planets," more commonly referred to as

The Public's Need to Know

Back in the economic depression of the 1890s, a local Beaver City couple struggled to feed their young child. They must have been successful, because by the age of two their darling daughter weighed 100 pounds. That's literally off the chart—the National Center for Health Statistics Weight-for-age Percentile for Girls chart.

The parents decided to have their daughter carry her own weight, as it were, when they put her on ten-cent-per-view exhibit on Decoration Day in 1896.

★ ★

asteroids. He is the first Nebraskan to have officially discovered an asteroid; he has been so proficient in his discoveries that no one is likely to catch up to his work anytime soon.

While any night-sky discovery takes awhile to gather subsequent verifying independent sightings, it's the original observer who gets the honor of naming the newly discovered asteroids. Lindholm has used his discoverer's prerogative to name these minor planets after Nebraska notables, such as Ted Kooser, Mari Sandoz, Doc Edgerton, Willa Cather, and even the state itself. In so doing, he's made his Lime Creek Observatory a national resource.

Lindholm is an uncommon Nebraskan. Not only can he find distant celestial bodies, but he also refrained from naming even one of them after a Husker sports figure. As if that weren't amazing enough in this state, when he's not wrapped up at night with his telescope, he spends time pursuing a raptor hobby, that of falconing.

The Lime Creek Observatory is about 15 miles north and west of Cambridge and about 4 miles west of the Medicine Creek Reservoir, also known as the Harry Strunk Lake.

The Artist's Name Was a Work of Art

Cozad

Not everybody is glad to be from Nebraska. Robert Henri hid his Nebraska origins for many years as he ascended the New York art world and became one of the most influential American artists in the early twentieth century. Henri was an artistic rebel and a guiding light of the Ashcan School, a group of realist painters who wanted to bring art down to street level in its representation of life.

Henri gave vague descriptions of his childhood, carefully avoiding any mention of Nebraska, and it took decades before researchers discovered his Cornhusker roots and his reason for dodging them. Henri's father was named John Cozad. John had left home as a child, traveled widely, and made a small fortune as a gambler. He invested much of his wealth in establishing a town named Cozaddale, near

★ ★

Robert Henri was the leader of a realist group of painters. Maybe that's why he didn't want people affecting the French pronunciation of his surname.
Robert Henri Museum

Cincinnati. The development flopped, so Cozad took his family—including his young son Robert Henry Cozad—west to Nebraska, where he founded a town on the 100th meridian (often cited as the longitude where the American West begins) named Cozad.

John Cozad bought 40,000 acres of land along the railroad tracks and built a hotel and a brickyard in his new community, then sold lots to settlers who built their homes from his bricks and stayed in his hotel until their houses were ready to occupy.

Cozad's reputation as a ladies' man and his success with the cards inevitably made him some enemies. But it was a disgruntled worker on one of his construction projects who assaulted him in a store one day, and Cozad shot the man with a gun he pulled from his boot. Knowing that angry residents might decide to take the law into their own hands, Cozad decided to make himself scarce. He packed up the family again and fled Nebraska.

John Cozad changed his name and even gave his son a new surname, claiming the boy had been adopted. When the family moved to the East Coast, Robert Henry Cozad went as Robert Earle Henri, and insisted it be pronounced the French way, "Hen-rye." Even though his father was eventually cleared of the murder charge, Henri never reclaimed his true identity. He preferred to keep the truth a secret and let the world know him by a name that was invented, one that approximated reality, like a work of art.

Trivia

East is east and west is west. Cozad is the line between them.

★ ★

Cozad's Robert Henri Museum is open from Memorial Day through September. It's located at 218 East Eighth Street (a mile north of I-80 exit 222). For more information, call (308) 784-4154 or go to http://roberthenrimuseum.org.

Getting Down on the Funk-Odessa Highway
Funk

Seven miles east of Holdrege, the town of Funk sits in a broad topographic depression of reasonably productive farmland. It's a plain, small town with hardworking people making a modest living from the land. Sigh . . .

The town got its start in the 1870s, when P.C. Funk convinced the railroad to establish a townsite beside the tracks. That was the good news; the bad news was they didn't locate the town near his land. Sigh . . .

There's a reason you were warned not to pick up hitchhikers on the Funk-Odessa Highway: They might be too funky to fit in your car.

* *

Funk had bright prospects in the early 1900s, but a series of fires devastated the town. Drought stunted the corn, then grasshoppers and locusts chewed the stalks down to the nubs. The Great Depression strangled cash flow and job opportunities. After World War II, the worst flood in Nebraska history rotted every building in sight. Sigh . . .

But the tide began to turn when construction of I-80 created temporary jobs and a high-speed route to a new life in Lincoln or Denver. This is when the Funk-Odessa Highway gained special meaning as the path of least resistance and the most direct route into the unknown. Undertones of mystery and misery attached to the highway after two high school girls picked up a melancholy hitchhiker one misty night. He told a haunting tale of despair from the darkness of the backseat. When one of the girls turned to ask if they could somehow be of help, she discovered the hitchhiker had vanished and they were alone in the car.

This legend added to the Funk-Odessa Highway's cachet among the young, who spoke of a depressed person as being "on the Funk-Odessa." A band from Holdrege penned a song called "FunkOdessa Highway Blues," which enjoyed brief popularity on radio stations in McCook and Kearney. The song was a brave attempt at merging the styles of Parliament-Funkadelic and Glenn Campbell.

At its philosophical core, the Funk-Odessa Highway represents good old-fashioned Nebraska values, like persistence despite all odds, low-grade depression in the face of those odds, and a gnawing sense that there is a way out—a path to a better life—but we're not about to take it because we don't want to mess up what we've already got, which may not be much, but it's darn predictable.

Funk's older crowd doesn't quite get the Funk-Odessa phenomenon, but these Baby Boomers have a little fun of their own with the town's suggestive name. Down at the grain co-op office, the receptionist will sell you a Funk University T-shirt with its elaborate official logo and simple slogan, "Funk U.," for only $18.

The Midland Co-op is located in downtown Funk on US 34/NE 6. For more information, call (308) 263-2441.

Long Time, No Sea

Millions of years ago, several eons after Pangaea broke into several continents and well before the Kansas State School Board decided the world is only a few centuries old, the grass-covered sand dunes of central and western Nebraska lay at the bottom of an enormous water body called the

Kevin Pope

Great Inland Sea. Then waters receded, mountains rose to the west, and the winds shifted the sands. Over millennia, this process created the largest underground aquifer in the world (not for long, at current rates of irrigation). Locals like to tell each other that our ocean has simply become too shallow for its beaches, much like the bald guy who claims he has grown too tall for his hair.

Well, this underground ocean is getting shallower daily. With so many center pivots sucking water from the High Plains Aquifer, you might think irrigators intend to reconstitute the inland ocean. Just in case, Nebraskans have prepared themselves for this possibility with the creation in 1931 of the Great Navy of the State of Nebraska. Since its inception, governors have recruited citizens and noncitizens alike to become Admirals in the Nebraska Navy. The certificate bestowing the honor says, in part, " . . . I [the Governor of Nebraska] do strictly charge and require all officers, seamen, tadpoles, and goldfish under your command to be obedient to your orders as Admiral—and you are to observe and follow, from time to time, such directions as you shall receive, according to the rules and discipline of the Great Navy of the State of Nebraska."

★ ★

Oh, Yeaahh!

Hastings

There are plenty of reasons to visit Hastings, but only one reason to make a pilgrimage. Hastings is the holy city and home of Kool-Aid, the drink that quenched a nation's thirst for more than three decades beginning around 1930. Add in a slab of Wonder Bread and a bowl of Jell-O, and you've got the happy equivalent of civilian C rations. Hastings is where it all started.

If he had been born a generation or two later, Edwin Perkins might have teamed up with Timothy Leary to manufacture some really far-out chemical compounds. Instead, he concocted the drink that served as a mixer for Leary's psychedelics (and Rev. Jim Jones's suicide cocktail). Long before those guys gave it a bad name, Kool-Aid was America's favorite low-cost family drink. In the late 1920s, Perkins adapted

What's your impression of this American icon?

★ ★

Kool-Aid from a liquid concentrate he called Fruit Smack. When the Depression hit, this 5-cent package of powdered, flavored concentrate was among the few affordable treats for kids. Street-corner Kool-Aid stands proliferated, and America settled into a decades-long love affair with this most generic of soft drinks.

Perkins was a nerdy kid with a chemistry set when his family lived in the village of Hendley, 100 miles southwest of Hastings. His father operated the general store, and Edwin cooked up a number of scented or flavored items for sale. As an adult, he developed a small mail-order business around a smoking cure called Nix-O-Tine, and moved with his new wife to Hastings as the business expanded. They invented Kool-Aid there in 1927. Kool-Aid's popularity soon swamped their production capacity, so the Perkins clan moved to Chicago, where a million packages of Kool-Aid flew out the factory door every day by 1950.

Carbonated soda pop eventually eclipsed the simpler delights of Kool-Aid. By the time Tom Wolfe wrote *The Electric Kool-Aid Acid Test* in 1968, the drink had been marginalized and culturally re-branded as the perfectly synthetic complement to LSD and other mind-bending substances. The People's Temple cult suicide in Jonestown, Guyana, in 1978 drove another nail in Kool-Aid's coffin by inspiring the saying, "They've drunk the Kool-Aid," as a reference to people who buy into a line of thinking uncritically. However, investigation of the Jonestown massacre revealed that a cheap knockoff called Flavor Aid may have been the actual product used in that unfortunate event.

You can forget about all that and relive the halcyon days of Kool-Aid every year during the second weekend of August, when Hastings rolls out the red carpet as it celebrates Kool-Aid Days. It's a wonderful time to join with others who still love the drink so much that they aren't afraid to drink the Kool-Aid.

The Hastings Museum of Natural and Cultural History includes a Kool-Aid exhibit. The museum is located at 1330 North Burlington Avenue. For more information, call (800) 508-4629 or go to www.hastingsmuseum.org.

★ ★

Dave's Personal Red-light District
Hastings

Dave Stewart takes the long view of life. When he started taking art classes at Hastings College, he gave himself fifteen years to prove up as an artist or move on to something else. He had no particular interest in art, but the perks of his custodial job at the college included free attendance at classes. So Dave took an art class, then another. He gravitated toward something called "assemblage art," which is like breathing new life into stuff you find in the Dumpster. Dave's always been something of a pack rat and junk collector, and now he's an icon in the local art scene, partly because he has marvelously merged his art with his nostalgia for the past.

Dave's home, his art studio, and his underground museum are all in the same building across the street from the old Burlington Railroad terminal in downtown Hastings. During World War II, the ground floor of the building served as a liquor store, while upstairs was a rooming house for soldiers and traveling salesmen. Above that, ladies of the night ran a bordello. It was an entrepreneurial trifecta.

Dave is the perfect owner and denizen of a building like this. His first-floor studio/gallery is a treasure trove of odds and ends—vintage radios and scrapped typewriters, pinup calendars overlooking old cigar boxes filled with ancient trinkets—and you sense a tenuous order in its chaos. It's the assembly line for his shadow box assemblages, where all manner of rescued stuff is within arm's reach.

A climb up a ramshackle staircase gets you to the third-floor museum, which is a wonderful homage to its former life as a house of ill repute. Dave has spared no imaginative expense in the luxurious re-creation of the bordello, and the fruits of his scrounging abilities are in full bloom in every detail of the bar, the sitting room, and the several bedrooms of this lascivious hideaway. From period wallpaper and fleshy portraits of buxom women to scantily clad mannequins staring at themselves in the mirrors above mother-of-pearl dressing

Dave breathes new life into found objects.

tables spread with jewelry and makeup, the dimly lit bordello rooms offer an exquisite peek at the sexual underworld of another era.

Dave doesn't charge admission, but you have to find him to arrange a viewing. It is well worth the search, and while you're there, have a

★ ★

chat with Dave. He's an accessible guy with a twinkle in his eye, and his Burlington Rooms historical site is a collage of love that only the fervid mind of this former plumber and custodian could produce.

Dave's art studio and gallery are located at the southwest corner of First Street and Denver Avenue (enter from the rear of the building). It's best to call first, (402) 463-1296.

You! Go Long and Put Your Hands Out
Hildreth

Let's say you live in a football-crazed state, but your high school only has thirty-four kids. Even if you could afford eleven uniforms, pads, and helmets, you can't field a complete team—even if you coerce the snot-nosed runt with Coke-bottle glasses into playing. So what do you do? Well, you do something most urban Americans are not much good at—you downsize. That's what Coach Stephen Epler did for the first time in American history back in 1934, at a time when downsizing was all the rage. Epler taught at the high school in Chester, Nebraska, and he was determined to get his students on the field. The result was six-man football, a free-for-all version of the larger gridiron game.

Six-man football became a phenomenon in sparsely populated areas of the plains states. It takes advantage of the best thing about growing up in a small town and going to a small school: Everybody gets to do everything, and you don't have to take steroids to be competitive. Here's how *American Boy* magazine described the beauty of the six-man game in the 1930s:

"In the older [eleven-man] game, the center, guards, and tackles carry much of the drudgery of the game while the ends and backs make the scores and get the cheers and headlines. In six-man there are no drudge jobs. Everybody carries the ball! Everybody scores! The glory and the fun are passed around."

Six-man games tend to have high scores, and teams have been known to quit and go home when scores get too lopsided. That must be what led to what's known as the "slaughter rule." It's a mercy killing that ends the game if one team gets ahead by at least 45 points after the first half.

A dozen Nebraska schools still tough it out in the state's six-man league—teams like the Greeley/Wolbach Titans and the St. Edward Beavers. But statewide fiscal pressures are putting the squeeze on small schools, forcing them to consolidate. This may ultimately slaughter the league along with some of its schools. It's that downsizing thing again.

You Can't Buffalo Me into Saying "Bison"
Kearney

Buffalo buffalo Buffalo buffalo buffalo buffalo Buffalo buffalo.

According to several revered grammatical sources, that particular list of eight repetitions of the same word above represents a structurally valid, complete sentence.

How is this possible? Well, you need three things: 1) a place called Buffalo (in this case, Buffalo County in the Bottom Lands of Nebraska), 2) an animal referred to in both the singular and plural as a buffalo, and 3) the verb "to buffalo."

In order to make the sentence understandable, you could substitute Nebraska for the place name Buffalo, change the animal buffalo to bison, and add a couple of words to restate the sentence thusly:

Nebraska bison [who] Nebraska bison bully [also] bully Nebraska bison.

Now work your way back to the original:

Buffalo [County] buffalo [who] Buffalo [County] buffalo buffalo [also] buffalo Buffalo [County] buffalo.

And finally:

Buffalo buffalo Buffalo buffalo buffalo buffalo Buffalo buffalo.

All of this buffaloing around is a way of introducing Ted Turner, owner or former owner of the Atlanta Braves, CNN, and more acreage than any other private landowner in Nebraska and in the nation.

★ ★

The *Omaha World-Herald* reports that Ted Turner owns one out of every twelve acres in the state.

Ted's property preeminence in cow country creates constant conversational commotion at local coffee shops. Rumors abound of likely land sales to Ted. Some suggest he is scheming to buy up water rights. Others believe he's cooking up a scheme to create his own privately owned buffalo preserve, reminiscent of a time when four-footers prevailed on the prairie. And with a herd of 40,000 of these beasts wandering his land, who's to argue?

Kearney is the Buffalo County seat and worthy of a bronze prize.

If You're So Smart, Why Ain't You Rich?

Ted Turner is one of America's richest men. He owns one twelfth of Nebraska's real estate, but even that doesn't impress folks around here. That's because of Warren Buffett, who is currently the richest man in the world. Mr. Buffett is Nebraska's proverbial hometown boy made good, the renowned Oracle of Omaha, the voice of reason in economically bumpy times.

Mr. Buffett still lives in Nebraska. There's got to be something going on to bring the kind of people who could afford to live anywhere in the world to live and vacation here.

If you're not living in Nebraska, perhaps you're saving up for the move?

A Monumental Arch
Kearney

The idea made perfect sense to the Kearney town fathers: build a new, impossible-to-miss tourist trap smack-dab in the middle of a mind-numbing stretch of interstate between Chicago and Denver. With eleven million cars speeding through each year on their way to somewhere else, just collecting the coins stuck between seat cushions could fund Kearney's annual budget. All they had to do was stick something so massive in the path of traffic that folks would stop either out of fear or curiosity. The rest is easy: The traveler places an $8 entry fee into the outstretched hand of a smiling cashier in exchange for a well-practiced "Howdy, Pardner" and a brochure.

Kearney boosters took a tip from the pre-Lady Bird highway beautification ethic of other roadside colossi (see Dr. Karal Ann Marling's

★ ★

*The Colossus of Roads: Myth and Symbol along the American High-
way)* dotting the US tourist landscape and hired designers to create
this "double-wide in the sky." After lavishly paying a consultant for
vague advice, this prefab landmark and museum was built next to the
interstate. Then, under cover of darkness one night in 1999, the $60
million, 1,500-ton arch was propped up over the freeway and dedicated to generations of American road warriors.

The arch was designed to bring motorists to a standstill halfway between Boston and San Francisco. Strange then that the first
improvement made after it opened was to install road signs on the
shoulders of I-80 warning motorists not to stop—at least on the
shoulder of I-80. Just remember when you see the arch on I-80 to
keep moving—you'll need to take your pictures at 80 mph if you're
keeping up with traffic, with both knees holding the steering wheel in
place.

Inside the arch, the Old West expansion story is told as well as anywhere in the country, using surround sound, video, and automatons
similar to Disney's "Pirates of the Caribbean" ride. But we haven't
seen anything like the small display that describes the early days of
the automotive travel. It's reminiscent of the accommodations in *It
Happened One Night* with Clark Gable and Claudette Colbert. That's
when America's romance with the automobile began and shaped
the highway enterprises that have gradually degenerated into cookie-
cutter franchise outlets.

While the I-80 traveler cannot help but notice the arch's menac-
ing placement over the interstate, the darn thing doesn't even have
its own exit. Visitors are forced to double back if headed westbound
or exit before the monstrosity comes into view if headed east. Many
point to this lack of easy access as a reason for the disappointing
number of visitors compared to the expensive consultant's early predictions. In an effort to build broader interest in the arch, locals convinced President Clinton, in the final days of the final year of his final
term in office, to visit. It was his first and only trip to Nebraska, the

✦ ✦

Home to Nebraska's longest escalator. This arch has no rival.

only state he had not yet visited during his presidency. President Clinton visited the arch on Friday, December 8, 2000. Did his visit help? Who knows? A few years later, on June 27, 2003, the *New York Times* printed an article about the arch titled "A Nowhere Striving to Be a Somewhere."

The arch provides an unexpected advantage: a chance to learn how Nebraskans pronounce "Kearney." Passersby tend to pronounce it as though it rhymed with the body parts "ear" and "knee," which is how its namesake, Colonel Stephen Watts Kearny, pronounced his name. However, residents pronounce the first syllable as "car." That gives "Kearney Arch" a nice alliterative ring. It certainly trips off the tongue a little more smoothly than its formal title: The Great Platte River Road Archway Monument. It also makes it a great place to visit on International Talk Like a Pirate Day in September, as in, "Ahoy, me hearties. You'd be a scurvy lot not to travel a league to the Kearrrrney

★ ★

You Just Can't Buy Advertising Like That

The 1992 Clint Eastwood movie *Unforgiven* is set in fictional Big Whiskey, Nebraska. Little Bill Dagget (Gene Hackman) and English Bob (Richard Harris) haven't seen each other for a while, and among the pleasantries exchanged as they catch up is the following:

Bob: "What I heard was that you fell off your horse drunk and broke your neck."

Dagget: "I heard that one myself, Bob. Hell, I even thought I was dead 'til I found out it was just I was in Nebraska."

Arrrrch to fill your hold with the booty she guarrrds. Arrrrr." But don't take the piracy role too seriously, or the Admirals of the Nebraska Navy (honorary titles offered by the governor) could mobilize to protect this treasure.

Love it or hate it, the arch represents the most current version of similar arch-type monuments over an earlier transcontinental road, the Lincoln Highway, remnants of which lay in downtown Kearney and elsewhere in Nebraska. Omaha and North Platte both had a Lincoln Highway arch; Cozad still has one on the highway through town.

And hey, at least it's not a McDonald's, which is what Oklahoma did to the Will Rogers Memorial Highway at Vinita.

They Died with Their Boots On
Lowell

You've heard of Boot Hill, the generic name for a cemetery filled with outlaws, gunslingers, murderers, and their victims. Folks who lived fast and died with their boots on rest in these often-makeshift burial

Booting up on vista meant something entirely different back then.

★ ★

sites. Many are not properly marked, and others aren't authentic, which means they aren't full of wild westerners or their residents weren't killed with sufficient violence to merit the title. Or the cemetery isn't on a hill.

The Boot Hill cemetery near Lowell qualifies on every count. It's on a hill overlooking an empty stretch of prairie. It was the scene of a vicious gun battle, although the participants were good, hardworking pioneers. But they had competing visions of pioneer life—ranchers wanted the prairie to remain open for cattle grazing,

Even the Liberals in Nebraska are Republicans

Just in case you're not sufficiently impressed by McCook's prodigious output of Nebraska governors, there is another hometown boy whose political career eclipses that of any other Nebraska politician (with the possible exception of William Jennings Bryan). George Norris served in the US House from 1902 to 1913, then spent thirty years in the US Senate.

Known as "the fighting liberal," Norris quarterbacked a Congressional revolt that created the modern seniority system in Congress. He was the father of the Tennessee Valley Authority and rural electrification in America. He pushed for single-house state legislatures, but only his home state took him up on the idea. John F. Kennedy called him the most important US senator in history.

Norris's home in McCook is at 706 Norris Avenue, just a block up the street from the Sutton House.

while homesteaders wanted to plant crops and fence the prairie for agriculture.

Between 1870 and 1876, this land use dispute got ugly. Dozens of people were killed in confrontations between farmers and ranchers. Twenty-six victims of these "range wars" are buried on Boot Hill, which is hard to find but worth the investigation. When you head south at the Gibbon exit, the pavement ends at an historical marker for the town of Lowell, which, like many small towns in Nebraska's past, vanished without much of a trace. Keep on going and you'll find this monument to victims of an unsettling time in the settling of the frontier.

Perhaps it's appropriate that the cemetery is fenced, but it also looks out on vast acres of open country.

You can find Boot Hill if you take I-80 to the Gibbon exit (exit 285), go 3.5 miles south to the pavement's end, then another 0.5 mile south to the T intersection, then east 0.5 mile, then a short distance south.

Little Prairie House on the Prairie
McCook

On its surface, McCook looks like any other small ranching and farming hub town. But there's something going on here. Maybe it's the fresh prairie air or an unusual combination of minerals in the drinking water. There has to be some reason why no fewer than three of Nebraska's governors were reared in McCook. Governors Ralph Brooks (1959–1960), Frank Morrison (1961–1967), and Ben Nelson (1991–1998) all earned their spurs in McCook before they headed out and made it to the top of the political heap in Nebraska.

If that fact is enough to make you want to steer clear of this community, please consider another unique facet of the town. Frank Lloyd Wright designed more than 500 buildings in his long and illustrious architectural career. Most of them are on well-worn paths through the urban landscape east of the Mississippi River. But should you

Mr. Wright's design is just right.

ever decide to visit the "lost homes of Frank Lloyd Wright," one of your first stops would be the Harvey P. Sutton home in McCook. It's the only Wright building in Nebraska, a classic two-story, stucco, wood-trimmed, prairie-style work of art by America's most celebrated architect.

One can only imagine how Harvey Sutton, a local jeweler, convinced Wright to design a home in western Nebraska. Who knows, it could have been because this prairie home is actually on the prairie! Or perhaps Wright had seen a performance of the Chicago, Burlington & Quincy Railroad Concert Band, of which Sutton was the director. The CB&Q Band was widely celebrated (at least on the Nebraska prairie), and Wright was a worldly guy. Seems obvious, yes?

Over the decades, the Sutton house, designed in 1905 and completed in 1908, changed hands and fell victim to some truly horrendous "improvements," like the cinder-block wall built around it, apparently reflecting a design style made popular by state prison systems. Fortunately, the home once again passed to more enlightened ownership and has been restored to its original beauty.

The Harvey P. Sutton House is located at the northwest corner of Norris Avenue and West F Street in McCook.

You Wouldn't Want to Mow This Yard
North Platte

There's no place on earth like Union Pacific Railroad's Bailey Yard in North Platte. It's a must-see for railroad buffs and quite a view of the world's biggest traffic jam on rails for anyone else. And should

Bring Out Your Dead

Points of Interest for Red Willow County (taken from a McCook tourism brochure):

Bartley Cemetery	Indianola Cemetery
Box Elder Cemetery	Nelson Bucks Massacre Site
Cedar Grove Cemetery	Pleasant Prairie Cemetery
Danbury-Marion Cemetery	St. Catherine Cemetery
Dry Creek Cemetery	St. John Cemetery
Fairview Cemetery	Trinity Cemetery
Hamburg Cemetery	Tyrone Cemetery
Hunting Area	Zion Hill Cemetery

Yard humping voyeurs observe from this tower.

you doubt the superlative nature of this spot, the *Guinness Book of Records* confirms that Bailey Yard is indeed the largest rail yard in the world.

Where else can you watch 150 trains wrestle with 500,000 tons of freight each day? And this is the truly amazing factoid about the Bailey Yard—3,000 railcars are humped every day! Now do you understand why there are so many railroad enthusiasts in America? This requires a bit of explanation, and it has nothing to do with the mating habits of locomotives and cabooses. Bailey Yard is home to two "humping yards," where railcars are sorted and assembled into trains destined for points hither and yon. Four trains per minute are pushed up and over an incline, which allows them to roll slowly through the yard for sorting and coupling (don't go there) as trains are assembled. It's about as exciting as watching a bad golf match, but it's the nuts and bolts (stop it) of the continental freight distribution system.

The Bailey Yard—named for a former Union Pacific Railroad president—is also a major fueling and repair facility for U.P. It contains 315 miles of track, which is only possible because this "yard" is 8 miles long. Until recently, there really wasn't any way to get a good view of it, but a wonderful new visitor center designed to look like a railroad spike now rises eight stories above the plains and affords a panoramic view of the yards and surrounding countryside. The Golden Spike Tower and Visitor Center tells the story of North Platte's historic place in transportation history. All the major migration routes to the West followed the Platte River through here—the Oregon Trail, the Mormon Trail, the Overland Trail, and the Pony Express Trail. The railroad followed suit. It has been here since Nebraska became a state, and North Platte has always been a railroad town.

William "Buffalo Bill" Cody lived near the yard in the late 1800s and took his Wild West Show around the country by rail. During World War II, six million soldiers passed through on troop trains. The trains stopped for fuel and the soldiers were treated to sandwiches and coffee by local volunteers at the passenger depot's North Platte

★ ★

Canteen. The depot was razed in 1973, but the story of the canteen has been preserved in books and documentary films.

The Golden Spike Tower and Visitor Center at Bailey Yard is at 1249 Homestead Road (take US 83 north from I-80 to Front Street, then west to Homestead Road). For more information, call (308) 532-9920 or go to www.goldenspiketower.com.

Almost-petrified Artists Replicate Old Buildings with Petrified Wood

Ogallala

Ogallala is a proud cowtown with a shoot-'em-up history. One of the remnants of that past is Front Street, a block-long Old West building façade with shops, a restaurant, and a museum behind signs for a jail, an undertaker, and a "tonsorial palace."

It's a kitschy attempt at creating a sense of the town's history, but there is a hidden gem at the end of this block: the Kenfield Petrified Wood Gallery. Inside you'll find the delightful creations of twin brothers Howard and Harvey Kenfield. For more than forty years, the two have collected petrified wood, mostly from Wyoming and states farther west. They shave off tiny strips and fashion them into three-dimensional miniature replicas of Old West buildings. Some are for sale and some are displayed in the gallery, which fills two rooms behind the shop. The gallery also features an impressive assemblage of arrowheads, which the brothers scavenged from the local countryside many years ago before they got interested in petrified wood.

Get them talking and the brothers may show you a few of their more unusual items, like a foot-long piece of what they call "flexible sandstone." It's naturally occurring sandstone with mica interwoven throughout, which gives it the unusual ability to bend from side to side.

Don't wait too long to visit Harvey and Howard, because they're not getting any younger. The Kenfields have donated their private collection to the county's community foundation, so we trust it will be on display long after these artists have claimed their spot on Boot Hill.

★ ★

The Petrified Wood Gallery is located at 525 East First Street (east end of "Front Street"). For more information, go to www.petrified woodgallery.com.

Tusk, Tusk! Ole's Is for Dead Heads

Paxton

Everybody knows about Ole's Big Game Steakhouse and Lounge in Paxton, but that's no reason to avoid it. In fact, Ole's has the best of two worlds—a great spot to find a hefty meal of protein on the hoof, and a world-class zoo where you can walk right up to all kinds of exotic critters . . . because they're mounted on the wall. It's as though

What's on the other side of that wall? The game room.

Ole decided not to waste the front end of these animals after he butchered the back end for steaks and burgers.

At Ole's, you'll find representative victims of many species—some of which may be extinct by the time you get there. As a matter of fact, a science teacher from a nearby town takes natural resources students on a field trip to Ole's every year. The students are tasked with examining all of the 200-plus magnificent mounts, then iden-tifying the specimens that are on the International Union for Con-servation of Nature and Natural Resources (IUCN) list of endangered species.

There are African elephants, golden eagles, owls, giraffes, baboons, desert lions, inyalas, kudus, elands, and dik-diks. Ole trav-eled five continents to bring home trophies to his watering hole. Not mounted but displayed in 8x10 photos are famous movie stars and politicians who have visited the joint. There's even a shot of old Ole Herstedt himself.

The danger here is that you'll accidentally back into a tusk or ant-ler, so watch your step. Otherwise, this place is perfect for animal lov-ers. Ole's got 'em all on the wall!

It's not hard to get directions to Ole's from a friendly local, as it's been around since one minute after Prohibition ended. It opened at 12:01 a.m. August 9, 1933.

It's located at 113 North Oak Street (north of I-80 exit 145 in downtown Paxton).

For more information call (308) 239-4500 or go to www.olesbig game.com.

Fred Lost Face with His Wife
Sacramento

Not far from the village of Funk is the turnoff to Sacramento, which is nearly a ghost town with a disturbing ghost story. Pioneers headed west in the 1800s could find a meal, a drink, and a night's refuge at a Sacramento roadhouse, whose proprietor was named Fred.

★ ★

Too scared to go inside.

Fred was a very sociable guy. He particularly enjoyed the company of a prostitute named Goldie, which didn't make much difference to anyone except Fred's wife. An unforgiving woman, she greeted him with a butcher knife when he came home one night from a visit to Goldie. After she killed him, she rendered him almost unidentifiable by shredding his face before she dragged him across the yard and dumped him in the well.

It didn't take a whole lot of imagination to figure out what had led to Fred's demise, but his wife was never charged. The prostitute left town and maybe even found a new line of work.

Fred's establishment changed hands many times over the years. It served as a general store for a while and was home to a speakeasy during Prohibition in the 1920s. This history was celebrated when the Speakeasy Restaurant opened on the site decades later. Restaurant

employees reported strange happenings in the building, including doors shutting inexplicably, knives that disappeared from the kitchen drawer, and the strange reflection of a man in mirrors, a man who wore a checkered shirt but had no face.

This faceless man has even been seen hitchhiking along the highway at night. No one ever stops to give him a lift. It may seem cruel, but let's face it, neither would you.

The Speakeasy Restaurant is located at 72993 S Road (6 miles southeast of Holdrege at the intersection of Polyline and S Roads). Call (308) 995-4757 or (308) 995-8545 for reservations.

Cowboys Weren't Their (Only) Enemy

Trenton

Ranchers and homesteaders flocked to Indian country in the mid-1800s and appropriated tribal lands because, well, they looked pretty empty. This de facto transfer of ownership happened unceremoniously over several decades. There's not much point in trying to salve our guilty collective memory of this period, but it should be noted that white interlopers weren't the only ones who drove off the Indian nations—they were pretty busy harassing each other, too.

The Pawnee were once the most powerful tribe in Nebraska. As whites inevitably moved west, tribes had to choose whether to fight, flee, or accommodate the endless stream of newcomers. The Pawnee chose accommodation and relied on the cavalry to protect them from their aggressive Sioux neighbors to the north and west.

In July 1873, around 700 Pawnee left their reservation in the Loup Valley for the annual buffalo hunt. A month later, they were camped along the Republican River near the present-day town of Trenton. On August 5, they headed up a nearby canyon despite warnings from white hunters who said Sioux warriors might be waiting for them.

The Sioux regularly attacked Pawnee hunting parties, but the Pawnee had promises of government protection, and whites were known to try to scare the Pawnee away from good hunting areas. So the

★ ★

Pawnee ignored the warning and proceeded up the narrow canyon, where Sioux warriors lay in wait. The Sioux attacked from both sides of the canyon, and the Pawnee, realizing they were vastly outnumbered, retreated to protect the women and children who followed behind. More than seventy Pawnee were killed before the Sioux abandoned their attack.

A spire to commemorate the expired.

★ ★

The Pawnee were thoroughly demoralized by the massacre. For years they had tread a difficult path between the intrusions of white settlers and the depredations of other tribes. What became known as the battle of Massacre Canyon marked the end of their annual buffalo hunt (and the last intertribal battle in Nebraska). A few years later, the Pawnee voluntarily resettled in the Indian Territory of Oklahoma.

The Massacre Canyon monument—a towering granite shaft erected by the federal government—commemorates this tragic moment in Pawnee history. Massacre Canyon also contains an archaeological site with remains of a prehistoric people (related to the Pawnee) who inhabited the Republican Valley between A.D. 500 and 1000.

The Massacre Canyon monument is located 3 miles east of Trenton on US 34/NE 6.

North Central

Anybody can love the mountains, but it takes soul to love
the prairie.

> Old Nebraska Sodbuster Saying
> as attributed on the Taylor, Nebraska, Web site.

*T*he Sand Hills represent a geology all their own. Writers often
wax poetic about the subtle beauty of the plains, with their
gently rolling hills, and their treeless vistas, and their miles and
miles of miles and miles. But they are talking of the high plains, not of
the Sand Hills. The Sand Hills are geographically unique in the entire
western hemisphere.

Traveling in the Sand Hills is different from travel in the High Plains,
and therefore in the mind-set of most visitors to the region. The dune-
ish hills prevent one from seeing the curvature of the earth because
here one doesn't travel straight ahead on a frozen rope highway. The
highway alternatively rises and falls between the upper portions of the
hills and the richly vegetated valleys, which are often too difficult to
plow. This is not the part of the plains that seems worn down by constant winds and weather to a smooth, grass-covered pasture for bison
and cattle. If the overused metaphor "a sea of grass" is to be applied
here, the grass must be planted on a boiling sea of hills, or on a tsu-
nami of bluffs.

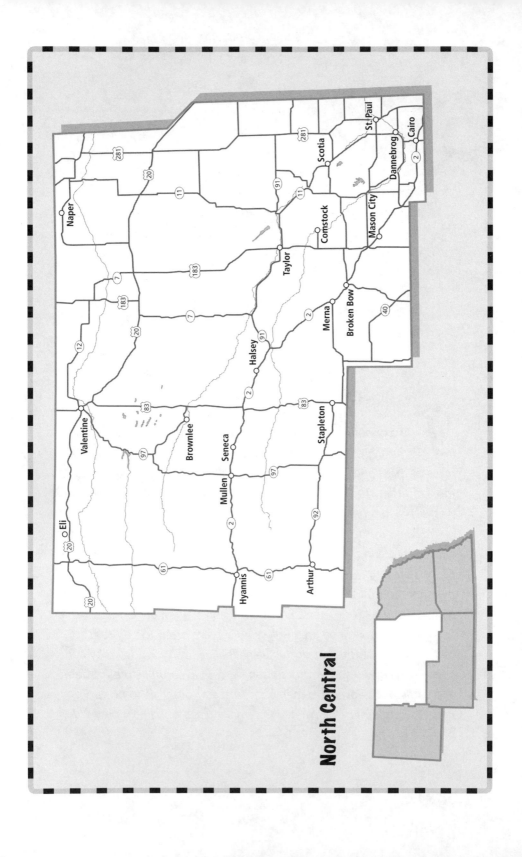

North Central

Towns are small, and the distances between them grow larger with each increase in the price of fuel. This is where the urban influences give way to the rural. No nature deficit disorder here—this is where people pay good money to hop on a horse or ride down the river in a horse tank to experience a reality that television has long ignored.

Metro-Nebraskans need their access to this part of the state. Those urban residents represent over half of the state's population; for them this is what is meant by "out West."

★ ★

What the Hay?

Arthur

One might expect the least populated county in the state to excel in minutiae. Arthur doesn't disappoint.

In 1928 the Pilgrim Holiness Church was built in Arthur out of baled rye straw. Many who speak of it today call it the "Hay Bale Church," but in fact straw makes a much better building material than hay. You can't tell by looking; the stucco on the exterior and interior camouflage the structure. If you get the key and go indoors, you'll notice that the walls are thicker than normal. This church is the only one of its kind constructed in the world.

It's doubtful the church builders were thinking of terms like "green building" or "sustainability," which are used to advocate straw bale construction for homes and other buildings today. They most likely built with the materials available to early farmers on what was mostly a treeless prairie. Maybe someday ranchers will come around to Ted Turner's thinking and concentrate on herds of bison. Before too long, they may even give up their four-wheelers and start riding horses.

There's another small building in this, the fifth least populated county in the country, worth your attention: the historic courthouse. Its one-room construction was befitting the smallness of the county, but eventually the county records outgrew the size of the building, and in 1962 the current courthouse was built. It's not very big, either, but a Taj Mahal in comparison to the one that served the county from 1914 to 1962.

Neither of these historic buildings could hold a bus tour if it dropped into town, not even if the tour group decided to split up.

The bank isn't very big, either, and probably doesn't have to be. But there are small banks aplenty in small towns. The small church and tiny local government complement each other in ways other county seats outgrew decades ago.

How much religion and government does a person need out in these wide-open spaces, really?

* *

A Head of the Headlines
Broken Bow

. . . the horns of the righteous shall be exalted.

Psalms 75:10

The town of Broken Bow undoubtedly has many claims to fame, but none is as compelling as Horace Easterwood, a hermit who lived somewhere north of town. Horace had a good reason for his excessively shy and retiring character, embodied in a horrible local secret that spilled onto the world stage—wouldn't you know it—when the *National Enquirer* plastered its pages with news that Horace had been born with a horn smack-dab in the middle of his head.

The Hope of Audacious

It's just a scattering of farmsteads north of Seneca now, but once upon a time Brownlee was part of a blossoming African-American farm community. Clem Deaver worked for the railroad in Seneca in 1904 when he heard rumors of available homestead land nearby. He rode up to the government office in Valentine, filled out the paperwork, and came back the proud owner of an acreage along the North Loup River. Deaver urged other blacks to stake claims nearby, and before long dozens of black families resettled there.

The town was renamed Audacious, which proved ominously apt as crop failures gradually drove farmers of all colors out of the Sand Hills. The ground was much better suited to ranching than farming, and as homesteaders abandoned their dreams of abundant agriculture, ranchers moved in with their cattle.

★ ★

Was this another wild supermarket tabloid allegation? Locals may not have appreciated the outing of their horned hermit, but they didn't deny the evidence held by the local hospital in the form of an X-ray of Horace's head, horn and all. To the credit of Broken Bow's population, they did not shun or scorn the deformed hermit. No, they tried to make him feel at home, perhaps even going overboard a bit by establishing an annual celebration of their hometown hermit. The mayor declared February 16 as Horace Easterwood Day in Broken Bow, and residents got into the spirit with a festival of gregarious events that included Horace T-shirts, kissing contests, and a giant hug that had to be discontinued after several people collapsed in the crush of affection for lack of breath.

Proceeds from Horace Easterwood events were donated to the hospital, along with contributions sent in by compassionate folks from communities near and far. The name of this man who lived in intentional obscurity now graces a list of donors on a plaque in the hospital's new wing.

Donations to a good cause should never be regretted, but our research determined that the alleged X-ray of Horace's head was actually ginned up by a nurse and an X-ray technician, who used a cow horn and a skull of undetermined origin for the official medical image of Horace's cranium.

If Horace Easterwood didn't really have a horn, did Broken Bow's beloved hermit even exist? You can decide for yourself, but there is a monument to Horace in the Broken Bow vicinity. Its location is not known. Horace would have wanted it that way.

Sandlubber or Landlubber?
Cairo

Some places are impressive for their civic achievements or recreational splendor. Others just plain don't have much to offer and are better left unnoticed. But there are still a precious few secret spots along the trail that are pregnant with unrealized opportunities. Cairo, Nebraska,

The metallic dromedary sounds like a good band name, doesn't it?

belongs in this category. If you do nothing else in life, you should consider standing at the corner of Suez and Egypt Streets in Cairo, Nebraska, and imagine the possibilities. This hamlet is filled with street names like Medina, Mecca, and Thebe. If ever there was a spot in the Sand Hills that's primed for a Sahara-style theme park, this is it. The local chamber of commerce (if they have one) has a little ground to make up—the town's name is pronounced "kay-ro," but that could be fixed through a civic pronunciation initiative. Residents have already felt the primal urge to celebrate the town's Egyptian roots by producing one camel sculpture, placed prominently at the ball park. Come on, Cairo, you've got the framework for a killer tourist trap; now let's see a few rides and snack food stands! How about a camel caravan trudging through town?

★ ★

The Music's in the Wind
Comstock

Nestled on the rising eastern bank of the Middle Loup River, Comstock is not your ordinary Sand Hills ranching town. It bills itself as the youngest town in Custer County (founded in 1889), and it appears to have the most youthful attitude in the region. Visitors are welcomed by a lovely public garden at the town's edge, laid out along a labyrinth of stone paths. The Comstock Labyrinth is a playful oasis of New Age consciousness in a very pragmatic landscape. As is the Friendship Patio next to it, placed within the ruins of a brick house and delineated by remnant walls surrounding a slab floor. Decorated with

Peace park? The answer, my friend . . .

whimsical artwork and heartfelt quotations, Comstock's Friendship Patio blends art and history and brotherly love into a private, refreshing encounter. The patio and labyrinth are obviously community projects, or they wouldn't occupy such a prominent spot at the foot of Comstock's Main Sreet, suggesting that the city fathers and mothers here have a markedly different notion of community than most towns in the region, or the state, for that matter.

The best expression of Comstock's alternative attitude spreads out across a hill north of town, where dozens of restored windmills announce the 2nd Wind Ranch, host of an annual summerlong series of country, rock, and Christian music festivals. Started in 2000, the series attracted tens of thousands of concertgoers but ran into trouble in 2005 when one person died and scores were arrested for underage drinking. The ranch and festivals have a new owner, and the music series has been scaled back. But the wind still blows around Comstock, and thousands still trek to this music oasis in the middle of nowhere.

The ranch claims to have more water-pumping windmills (about 125) gathered together than any other place on Earth.

The 2nd Wind Ranch is 3 miles north and 1 mile east of Comstock. For more information, call (308) 728-3113.

Truth Lies Here
Dannebrog

He's not Danish and he says he's not really a baker, but Tom Schroeder is close to the heart of Dannebrog. He owns and operates the Danish Baker, a cafe and baked goods emporium on Main Street. He serves "heart attack" sandwiches for breakfast (egg on slab of cheese), only one choice for lunch (beans and corn bread), and on Thursday evenings he bakes as many as 200 best-in-the-world pizzas. There's nothing dainty about Tom's Italian cuisine. His large pizza pie is fully 5 pounds of meat and mozzarella.

★ ★

After the morning rush, the "Visitor Center," as the sign calls it ("it's where the best visitin' in town happens"), settles into coffee and nickel-ante Sheep's Head card games. The till is open on the counter, and regular card players pour their own coffee, grab a soda pop from the fridge, and make their own change when they pay on their way out. Tom bakes cookies in the afternoon and has a strict rule that if you're there when they come out of the oven, you get one free.

What's life like in Dannebrog's hot spot? On an average afternoon, an elderly man in overalls and a ball cap stitched with "Yer basic hat" might take a seat, set his cassette player on the table, and tell Tom he has to hear the man's granddaughter playing "Star Spangled Banner"

Visiting hours are when Tom is in.

Liar, Liar

Dannebrog's most famous resident is humorist Roger Welsch, whose "Postcards from Nebraska" segments aired on CBS News' *Sunday Morning* program for many years. Welsch founded the National Liars Hall of Fame, which started out as a convenient place to store some of his more unusual junk (a bag of "cowboy bubble bath," for example, which looks a lot like baked beans). In recent years, the collection has been lodged in a gift shop that used to be an embalming studio on the town's main street, where it features a collection of T-shirts and minor gag items. The Liars Hall has always been more about concept than concrete location, and by the time you read this, it may have disappeared altogether. Its most recent owner has moved to Arizona and put the Liars Hall up for sale.

In a less confident town, the possible loss of the Liars Hall might be cause for panic. Dannebrog is not that town. People seem pretty darn content with life here. It would take more than the demise of the Liars Hall to throw them off-kilter. Maybe the loss of the Danish Baker would do it.

on the violin. It becomes clear why he wants Tom to hear it when Tom pulls out his guitar and plays a couple of songs he wrote, one about a friend who died in Iraq and one about how much he loves his wife.

Lars Hannibal led the group of Danish immigrants who settled the town and gave it its unique name. Dannebrog is a Danish word denoting the national flag. It's the only town of that name in the world, and the state has designated it Nebraska's Danish Capital. A sign announces this distinction at the town's main intersection.

The Danish Baker is located at 114 Mill Street N. For more information call (308) 226-2208.

★ ★

Stone Cold Wood

Eli

You are reading this book, so we know you are a connoisseur of the unusual. But how far would you go, how hard would you search, and how odd would the discovery have to be to get you out on the back roads of Nebraska's wide-open ranchlands?

This spot could be the true test of your commitment to all things curious. It's the Conley Flat Cemetery, and it's so modest that it's difficult to find even when you get there. But it's worth it if you're the kind of person who wouldn't want to pass up a chance to see a

"Scared to death?" "Petrified!"

cemetery where the cemetery stones are not made of stone but of the next best thing in these parts—petrified wood.

These dry land Sand Hills offered neither abundant timber nor any ready supply of durable stone for grave markers. So a few sturdy Depression-era ranching families in these parts came up with suitable alternatives. Some unearthed slabs of petrified wood and carved them with the names of the deceased. Others fashioned cement markers with lettering formed from small pieces of multicolored glass.

It's a quaint and unusual touch in peaceful stretch of grassland.

The cemetery is about midway between Cody and Merriman, and about 8 miles southeast of Eli. The last 0.5 mile to the cemetery can be tricky after a rain shower, so choose your day carefully or wear rubber boots.

To get to Conley Flat Cemetery, head south, take the first left, and follow the road to the cemetery, which is fenced and identified. Best bet is to get directions at the grocery store in Eli.

Largest Hand-Planted Forest

Halsey

The grandest unnatural feature in the state is the largest man-made forest in the world; 20,000 acres (30-plus square miles) of timber planted beginning over 100 years ago. The concept was championed by conservation president Teddy Roosevelt back in 1902. Most of the planting was done during the Great Depression through the efforts of the Civilian Conservation Corps (CCC). The Halsey National Forest is home to Nebraska's one and only fire tower and to the oldest federal nursery, which is the birthplace of seedlings used to replant forest-fire-stricken portions of the United States.

That bears repeating for those who think of this part of the country as a barren plain: The Bessey Nursery in Nebraska is the birthplace of millions of seedlings used to replant forests across the nation. It's one of the reasons Nebraskans were for years known as Tree Planters, but that was back in a day when people wanted to be known for what they did more than which football team they liked.

To enjoy the forest, take the time to drive in and hike around. If you are lucky enough to climb the fire tower, you might recall the

Cedar trees? Yup, I see der trees.

* *

story in Frank Herbert's classic science fiction adventure, *Dune*. In it the rebels planned to permanently change the arid planet by collecting enough water and applying it to transform the desert ecosystem into a more temperate one. Similarly this forest was to begin a timber industry that would support the lumber needs of the homesteaders for whom the lure of free land just wasn't enough.

The landscape certainly did change, but time may yet win it back. The native soil doesn't nurture unplanted seeds unless they are yucca, grass, or wildflower. If this century-old forest is to survive, it needs another tree-planting effort similar to that which created it. Consider the forest a memorial to the Arbor State, and offer to plant one when you visit.

If you visit, be sure to take a look at the oldest swimming pool on Forest Service land. It's an interesting historical view of recreational architecture, a throwback to a time when kids in town spent 25 cents at the Saturday matinee in order to cool off.

The National Forest entrance lies 2 miles west of Halsey on NE 2.

What's in a Name?

Hooker County

Hooker County doesn't need mentioning; it needs defending. It's a simple county—NE 2 is its only east-west road, and NE 97 is the one and only north-south thoroughfare. Their point of convergence is the county's only town, Mullen.

Here are four things you should know about Hooker County:

It's named after a Civil War general, so put the other possibility out of your mind.

Mullen is a modest, civil, God-fearing community; so again, keep any images of a Sand Hills Mustang Ranch to yourself.

There used to be signs at the county border saying WELCOME TO HOOKER COUNTY. They were stolen so often by people who collect such items that county authorities no longer post their welcome. You just have to believe they're glad to see you.

★ ★

The state legislature once considered putting county names on all license plates as an identifier. The legislator representing Hooker County begged his colleagues not to subject his constituents to the mockery they would have to endure if they had to drive around the state with "Hooker" prominently displayed at the bottom of their license plates. The legislature got a good laugh out of the matter and then dropped the proposal.

The county may not have much except good ranch land, but it's got plenty of that. In fact, the land is good enough to have attracted Nebraska's largest landowner—Ted Turner—who is swallowing ranches faster than you can say, "Saddle 'er up!"

If Ted Turner comes as a surprise to the county, so do the two world-class golf courses. The exclusive Sand Hills Golf Club benefited from Ben Crenshaw's involvement in the design, and it features one of the top twenty courses in the world. Not far away is the newer Jack Nicklaus project, the Dismal River Golf Club, a similarly exclusive affair catering to folks who can afford to arrive by private jet. It must be quite a sight in this laid-back cattle country. But in a place called Hooker County, you learn to expect the unusual.

Ups and Downs
Hyannis

Many Nebraska towns are named after places farther east where our settlers originated. Peru, Oxford, and Prague are examples. Some are named after famous people, like Red Cloud, Seward, and Fremont. Others may be linked more to a state of mind—take Funk, Wahoo, or Republican City, for example. Hyannis, Nebraska, is in the first category, as it was named for its founder's hometown in Massachusetts.

Hyannis sits in the midst of the Sand Hills and some of the finest cattle-grazing land on the planet. Cowboys on the earliest cattle drives out of Texas discovered both the austere beauty and the productivity of this region. They christened it "God's own cow country"

and immediately began fighting over it. Indians got involved too, since it was technically theirs to start with.

When all was said and done, a handful of families controlled most of the ranchland, with individual holdings as large as 300,000 acres. Many of these super-charged cowpokes lived in the hamlet of Hyannis, making it the wealthiest community in America for many years around 1940. Since then, some have left the area after realizing that—in a county where cattle outnumber humans by about 100,000 to 1—things could get rough if the cattle ever got disgruntled and did the math.

Up, Up, and Away

Hyannis has an indirect link to the history of aviation in America. Chris Abbott was one of the most successful ranchers and businessmen in Hyannis. He was said to be the richest person in Nebraska in the 1940s, with huge cattle and land holdings as well as banking and business interests across the state.

Aviation was one of his interests. He started Prairie Airways in Lincoln and an aircraft fueling company called Rocket Air Service in Omaha. His second wife—Ethel Abbott—had previously been a co-owner of the Lincoln Aircraft Company, which operated a pilot training school. A twenty-year-old from Wisconsin walked into the school one day. He had never touched an airplane before, but he wanted to begin flight training. His name was Charles Lindbergh.

Ethel Abbott kept in touch with Lindbergh over the years, and he sent her a telegram from Paris after his historic transatlantic flight.

★ ★

Wealth comes and goes. In 2002 the US Census Bureau stated that Grant County, of which Hyannis is the county seat, was one of the poorest counties in the nation. It wasn't alone; that year Nebraska had five of the poorest twelve counties.

These things have a way of changing; in 2006 Nebraska had only two of the poorest ninety-one counties in the United States. The thing is, in order to spend all that extra cash, one needs to leave the county!

Hyannis is midway between Thedford and Alliance on NE 2, and 70 miles north of Ogallala on NE 61.

PDA: Public Display of Artistry

Mason City

Richard Martin lived for a long time in Mason City. He blended in pretty well, which means he worked for the railroad, paid his taxes, and went to church on Sunday. In fact, he helped with construction of the church that stood catty-corner from his house.

Dick liked to keep busy, even after he retired. But with the new church completed and his home in good repair, what's a handy guy with a lot of practical skills and an artistic eye to do? Dick turned his capable hands to metal sculpture. Using recycled tractor seats, engine parts, vehicle wheels, flywheels, gears, and other discarded farm machinery, he welded all sorts of creatures. Some are from the animal kingdom; some resemble human forms; some were machined entirely in Dick's imagination. There are thunderbirds and Indian heads and giant insects. A skeleton wearing a Nazi helmet and riding a motorcycle points a machine gun at passersby under the gaze of a vulture. A black beetle whose shell used to be the hood of a Ford pickup graces the front lawn. There's a turkey, a roadrunner, an ostrich, a ladybug, and several critters of unknown species. It's a wondrous menagerie of junk metal and a personal tribute to the Midwestern tradition of fine yard art.

Dick died more than a decade ago, but his family seems committed to preserving his sculptures just as Dick arranged them. It must make mowing the lawn a little trickier, but this is one yard you wouldn't

The details of this work are a bit devilish.

mind spending time in. Some think Richard Martin's pièce de résistance stands on the corner, facing the church. It's a big red devil holding a pitchfork and smiling. The sculpture is titled "Dick's Dilemma."

The yard art is located at 708 Prentiss Street.

Bartak's Depression
Merna

In the mid-1990s an out-of-state geologist did some preliminary tests at a mile-wide depression on the Bartak farm near Merna. He made a pronouncement that caused a bit of a stir in the geological circles: He suggested that the early evidence indicated Bartak's Depression was

Get cratered, then depressed.

a crater caused by a meteor impact. Not many craters exist in North America, and one that happened so recently (around 3,000 years ago—fresh as today's eggs in astronomical impact terms) made both professional and amateur scientists take note.

Merna boosters perked up their ears at the news. Town celebrations had peaked a few years earlier for the centennial. They thought that adding a geographic attraction that could be loosely tied to circles out in the fields, or slogans like "Merna rocks" could entice a few more people and sell a few shirts.

But after the initial publication some University of Nebraska–Lincoln (UNL) scientists published their own opinion about the cause of the depression. Their opinion: The depression was formed by wicked winds on the prairie. Sand hills have for years been subject to such terrain-carving winds, leaving behind bare sand depressions known colloquially as blowouts. This one seemed a little larger than others, and a little older, too.

While the UNL and out-of-state thinkologists traipsed off to varying prestigious "what's the cause of this hole?" conferences to defend their views, Merna acted decisively. Local folks noted that a simple mis-spelling like Bartok's Depression could shift out-of-town conversation to the unproductive years of the composer's otherwise notable life, while Merna's Crater had the benefit of reminding people of the town name; it had impact. Their celebration became Merna Crater Days.

Whatever you call it, it's outside of town on private property. Ask for directions.

White Horse Ranch
Naper

Horses take time. They need to be fed, and if you don't work with them routinely, they tend to think of themselves as the center of the universe. They're a bit like small children that way.

This is still horse country, but the introduction of small all-terrain vehicles (ATV) has diminished the importance of horses. It takes less

Making an Impression

Local folklore has it that a young man who traveled by train through Merna on his way home to Montana thought so much of the name of the town that he suggested it to his wife as a name when they had a daughter. The Williams girl changed her surname to Loy when she was out in Hollywood; if you watch black-and-white murder mystery movies like the Thin Man series, you know they kept the sound but changed the spelling to Myrna.

★ ★

time to fuel up and start an ATV than it does to catch and saddle a horse; an ATV requires less care when not in use.

There are many stories about the diminished importance of horses today. Perhaps none is more telling than the guy who took his trailer with a couple of horses to a sale barn and didn't even unload them because he was told there wasn't a market for them. Feeling a little surprised, he hopped back in his truck to head home. When he opened the trailer to unload his cargo, he found an even bigger surprise: Someone had loaded another horse onto his trailer while he was in the sale barn. They can't even give horses away out here!

It wasn't always like this. There was a time when people could make a national name for themselves by working with horses. The White Horse Ranch was the best example in Nebraska. Sometime before World War II, Cal and Ruth Thompson got it in their heads that Nebraska needed some white horses—not white horses with black patches or a gray mane or an off-white tail, but pure white horses. So they dedicated themselves to breeding white horses on their ranch nestled in the Niobrara Valley near Naper. While they gradually developed their new breed, they also operated a riding school, where disadvantaged kids learned to ride the gorgeous critters and even train them.

A lily-white breed of horses evolved. So did a generation of darn good horse handlers. The Thompsons capitalized on all this talent by assembling the White Horse Troupe, which toured the United States with its demonstrations of exceptional bareback riding techniques on the pearly steeds. The show attracted crowds and enjoyed national attention during the 1940s and '50s. White horses from the Thompson ranch even appeared in Hollywood movies.

Unfortunately, the Thompsons were never able to secure a distinct breed designation, so the white horse breeding experiment failed along with the Thompsons' hope of selling breeders. Instead the ranch depended on entertainment revenues for survival. When Cal Thompson died in 1963, Ruth closed the show and the ranch. The marvelous white horses were sold or given away. For her success in

★ ★

working with children, Ruth Thompson was inducted into the Cowgirl Hall of Fame in 1990.

Three decades after the White Horse Ranch was put out to pasture, a young couple took it upon themselves to restore the ranch and bring back the white horses. It was a valiant effort, but the White Horse Ranch closed again in 2006 and the white horses rode off into the metaphorical sunset—this time for good.

The ranch is southeast of Naper, nestled between the confluence of the Keya Paha and Niobrara Rivers.

A Jarring Sight

St. Paul

Alice Osterman took a pottery class many years ago and produced a cookie jar for her grandmother. After Grandma died, the jar came back to her, and she displayed it on a shelf in her cafe, the Sweet

This collection is a load of crock.

Shoppe, in St. Paul. Somehow one cookie jar led to another and another, and now Alice is known for two things: her exquisite pies and her cookie jar collection. At last count, there were 1,085 jars lining tiers of shelves stretching around the two long rooms of her bustling cafe. Let's face it—a cookie jar collection is just another collection, but did you know that cookie jars come in the shape of a loaf of raisin bread? How about a gas pump or a cactus or a pair of cowboy boots or an Airstream trailer?

Alice once built a life-size cookie jar for a parade float. Her daughter played the cookie as they rode through town during Grover Cleveland Alexander Days, a July celebration of the area's most famous son. Alexander was a Hall of Fame pitcher who played Major League ball from 1911 to 1930. He still holds National League records for most shutouts and most career wins.

The Sweet Shoppe is located at 605 Howard Avenue. For more information call (308) 754-4900.

Chalk One Up for Happy Jack
Scotia

You've heard of the coastal Canadian province of Nova Scotia? Out here in the middle of Nebraska, there's a Scotia sans Nova and its tourism highlight, the Happy Jack Chalk Mine. Eat your heart out, Nova Scotia.

Trivia

St. Paul also gave birth to Dorothy Lynch salad dressing, which was dreamed up by a woman of that name (yes, there is a Dorothy Lynch!) who ran the restaurant at the Legion Club with her husband in the 1940s.

★ ★

Knowing that Happy Jack is one of only two underground diatomic mines in America and the only one open to the public, you may want to redraw the map of your next family vacation destination. As you prepare for this adventure, rest assured that you don't need any special masks or protective clothing to approach a diatomic mine. After all, "diatomic" means simply a molecule "composed of two atoms." That may not clarify much, but it shouldn't raise your health insurance premiums, because diatomic molecules are the most abundant molecules in nature. Many of them are homonuclear (and constitutionally protected), but that has nothing to do with how this particular chalk mine got its name.

Happy Jack is the name of the peak into which the chalk mine burrows. Jack may have been the soldier who discovered the ore deposit in the mid-1800s or one of the entrepreneurs who developed it as a working mine. The stone was first used as a building material, but when the lightweight stone melted in the rain and buildings collapsed into rubble . . . okay, that didn't happen, but at some point they found a better use for the chalk stone as an ingredient in paints.

Today the area is preserved for recreation and educational uses, with picnic tables, a hiking trail, and a wonderful view of the surrounding area from the peak. The Happy Jack Peak and Chalk Mine is a low-budget private enterprise, but it's worth a stop and a few moments of reflection on the importance of diatomic molecules in modern life.

The Happy Jack Chalk Mine is 2.5 miles south of Scotia on NE 11. For more information, call (308) 245-3276.

Time Travelers
Seneca

Remember the old Chicago song, "Does Anybody Really Know What Time It Is?" Well, the answer is no if you live in Seneca, 15 miles west of Thedford. Seneca has the singular misfortune to sit directly on the line dividing the Central and Mountain time zones. The town has

opted into one zone or the other, based on practical considerations.
Originally a railroad town, residents lived on Central Time because
that's how the railroad worked. When railroad jobs dried up, the pri-
mary concern became getting the kids to school on time. When the
local school merged into the school district based in Thedford, towns-
people followed Central Time to avoid confusion for the morning bus
ride. Years later, the school district decided to let students choose
between Thedford's school and the school in Mullen, 11 miles west
of Seneca in the Mountain Time zone. Chaos resulted from the duel-
ing clocks and ticked people off so much that now individual families
decide their time zone loyalties. The Cattleman's Restaurant operates
on Mountain Time, while the B&B on the next block takes in weary
travelers on Central Time.

The line dividing Central from Mountain Time in Nebraska effec-
tively dissolves when it enters Seneca and reconstitutes itself on the
other edge of town. While people in some towns face an uncertain
future, the uncertainty in Seneca starts with the present time.

How do locals feel about this?

"It's hell scheduling a meeting," says Larry Hardy, whose wife Nina
runs the Cattleman's Restaurant. "Everyone uses the time change to
their own advantage. If you miss a meeting, you say you were working on the other time."

Being an Outsider Is an Art
Stapleton

Life in Flyover Country isn't always easy; hardworking residents
believe it's one of the reasons people choose not to linger. The land
is unforgiving—if untended, its greenery will overtake the works of
man in a single season. Everyone here knows their job is to sweat and
toil in order to maintain the benefits of the sweat and toil of earlier
generations.

As you drive down the road, you'll pass at least one abandoned-
looking old farmstead; the long grass, broken fence, and peeling

Ride a Critter!

Sandy Hansen of Seneca doesn't really care which time zone she's in. She builds large wooden animals in her garage and ships them to forty-nine states and several foreign countries. Sandy has been a commercial seamstress for more than forty years. Her father gave her the inspiration for her animals, which are large enough for a child to ride and strong enough to hold a 300-pound man. He was down on his hands and knees one day, giving a ride to one of his grandkids. Never mind that he'd had two knee replacements.

Sandy was horrified and decided to build a riding horse for her child. One led to another, and now Sandy has a one-person assembly line that has cranked out more than 1,600 of these super-sturdy riding animals. Her business is called Critter Corral, and she gets most of her sales at rodeos and stock shows.

Granny's got your goat. Or horse. Or giraffe.

paint makes it look as though it hasn't had anyone living in it for years. In Hollywood horror tradition, a murder mystery lies within. But this isn't Hollywood. In one particular small wooden shed behind an unpainted house in this part of the state, the mystery was more wondrous than murderous.

Emery Blagdon once invited a local pharmacist to visit the shed on his farm to see his Healing Machines. Inside the gray peeling exterior, he turned on the string lights to reveal a multitude of wire sculptures in the middle of the room, with paintings stacked around the exterior.

★ ★

Emery had spent years crafting sculptures of baling wire, copper wire, tin foil, wood, plastic, and other found materials into machines that he felt channeled healing forces of nature. The paintings were part of the operation but did not hang on the walls; they were instead piled in strategic locations. Emery started making his creations in the mid-1950s when he was forty-eight. He continued his artistic endeavors until he died in 1986.

The local pharmacist made no medical judgment about the healing machines; pharmacies, after all, carry copper bracelets because customers demand them, not because doctors prescribe them. But this trip began an adventure for Blagdon's work that neither envisioned.

When Blagdon passed away, the pharmacist purchased the shed and the works inside it at the estate sale. Most who attended the sale saw the potential of the shed diminished by the work it would take to clear out all of the wire, plastic, wood, and tin foil and decided not to bid. But wrapped inside the shed in the dark lay a treasure of art.

Art is an insular world, not unlike rural Nebraska. When Blagdon's Healing Machines were introduced to the insiders of the art world, they were introduced as outsider or folk art. Blagdon's work has become as emblematic of outsider art as Andy Warhol's posters are of pop art.

Alas, you cannot usually view Blagdon's works here, nor are they held in Nebraska. The largest part of the collection is held in Wisconsin by the Kohler Foundation.

But you can take comfort in the knowledge that the sweat and toil hidden in a nondescript outbuilding in the middle of nowhere can house a personal vision of beauty that will excite a global community in ways the locals don't comprehend.

The Only Town Around
Taylor

Taylor may not appear in any tourist brochure, but it's a delight to see because of its playful and artistic celebration of its past. Evidence of a sense of history and style greet you as you arrive at the town square. Historic buildings have been moved to the square. Across the street, the Pavilion Hotel has had a face-lift. Local lore suggests this stately gathering place had a less-than-stately reputation in its heyday, thanks to a thriving red-light business. Each historic building features expertly designed life-size cutout figures peering in the window. These figures surprise you at every turn as you explore this gem of a village.

Taylor is the county seat, administrative center of the school district, and home of the county fair for the simple reason that it is the only incorporated community in the county.

Big Giant Hills

Sheridan / Cherry Counties (equidistant to Whitman)

The words "big" and "giant" are relative terms, and when we talk about the mountains in Nebraska . . . well, there aren't any. Colorado has mountains; we have hills. Mountains jut into the sky while hills only disturb the calm surface of an inland ocean suitable for prairie schooners. The Sand Hills are the state's most famously curvaceous countryside, but as hills go, they don't amount to much. In fact, the only hills in this part of Nebraska that merit a mention on the map are called "Giant Hill" and "Big Hill." Giant Hill sits about 10 miles north of Seneca, while Big Hill looms 60 miles to the west. These mini-mountains are notable for two reasons:

First of all, they indicate the straightforward approach to life that predominates in this ranching country. Early residents must have beheld Big Hill, commented on its altitude, and named it accordingly. Presumably these same name-givers stumbled onto Giant Hill at a later date and again noticed its stunning departure from the topographic norm. Since "Big Hill" was already taken, they opted for the first synonym they could think of without getting too flowery about the whole idea.

These early namers must have been a separate crew from those who actually measured the altitude of places. That's our other reason for identifying them as high points in the area. You see, Giant Hill rises 3,400 feet above sea level, which is just about tall enough to tip over the average Nebraskan for looking at it. Sixty miles to the west is Big Hill, which by all rights ought to be the smaller of the two, but rises to the dizzying height of 4,144 feet.

So there you have it—Big Hill is bigger than Giant Hill. If that's not enough to flummox you, consider this: The highest point in the state isn't even on a hill. It is a virtually unnoticeable spot on the state's southwestern edge where the land gently but persistently rises toward Colorado. It's a poor excuse for a high point, but then altitudes are not one of Nebraska's high points.

The two hills are about 3.5 hours driving distance apart; Whitman is closest to the halfway mark. Giant Hill is about 10 miles north of Seneca; Big Hill is about 30 miles north of Ashby close to the Sheridan-Cherry county line.

Star Light, Star Bright, Starry Night
Valentine

Nebraska, like the rest of country, has become more urbanized over the years. People speak fondly of wide-open spaces and personal freedom while they leave the farm and move to the cities in droves. House sizes have grown to McMansion size in expansive neighborhoods that swell the girth of metropolitan centers. Cities sprawl over surrounding countrysides, replacing cowpaths and corn with cement, shopping centers, and miles of streetlights, billboards, and a multiplicity of light sources demanding passersby to "Look! Look at me! Look at me!"

As each additional light elbows the others with its amped-up glare, the impact is one described by the International Dark Sky Association (What? There's an international advocacy association for darkness?) as light pollution evidenced by too darn much sky glow, light clutter, and associated decreased nighttime visibility. If the birth of both science and religion started with an examination of the night sky, is the death of each inevitable as more lights and more urban light pollution clutter and obscure the view of all but the moon and most brilliant stars?

Many subscribe to the view that television, computers, cars, and air conditioning have joined urbanization in delivering the unintended societal consequence known as nature deficit disorder. Not only do people not know where milk comes from (a carton, right?) but they also don't have any sense of what happens in the world without people.

People here know. Luckily for those Out West, the increasing dearth of population provides several added side benefits. Parking is easier to find. Lines at the grocery store aren't as long. Conversations happen more often as there are fewer people with whom to have them. And on a cloudless night, the sky is so full of stars that locals start to feel just a little bit crowded.

A generous nature exists among those who live so far out in Fly-over Country that they see nary a clue of a hint of an urban glow on the horizon. And they're ready to seize this modest black hole of opportunity and share their dark outlook on life by hosting the annual Nebraska Star Party in the Sand Hills outside of Valentine.

And why not throw a party in the dark and for the dark? Between the vast city centers of the country, people are scrambling to create "Dark Sky preserves," stray enclaves of worthwhile heavenly viewing among the spreading pools of overzealous lighting.

Attendance at the weeklong Nebraska Star Party numbers in the hundreds and is friendly to city dwellers and dark sky initiates, but they need to leave their lights at home.

It's worth your time. Just open up your electronic calendar and write down the week when the new moon is nearest to the last of July or the first of August. Be sure to check the brightness on that screen while you are at it.

The Star Party is held at the Merritt Reservoir, which is located 23 miles south and west of Valentine on NE 97. For more information, go to www.nebraskastarparty.org.

Love Post

Postmasters from around the country have plenty of stories to tell, and not just about the time they stayed open until midnight on April 15. There was a time when philatelic activities were recommended to the youth of America; they were just as often encouraged to take a look at the travels of their written correspondence by tracking postmarks.

I heart you!

Today, Facebook, Twitter, e-mail, and instant messaging have all made the likelihood of receiving a handwritten message delivered by the US Postal Service about as likely as a PETA award at the annual Cattleman's Ball.

Are you looking for a unique way to demonstrate your love? How about a heartfelt message from the Heartland, postmarked in Valentine, Nebraska's Heart City? The local postmaster, Arlene Paulson, is happy to help you. The post office in Valentine receives around 20,000 letters to be postmarked locally for Valentine's Day delivery, in a tradition going back about fifty years. They started using a new design in 2009. Just make sure those cards and letters are correctly addressed and have the right postage on them when you put them all in an envelope mailed to:

Postmaster
Valentine Remailing
Valentine, NE 69201

Be sure to get them in the mail so that Paulson receives them about ten to twelve days prior to expected delivery.

For those of you who chronically forget anniversary dates and birthdays, Valentine's Day is February 14. Every year. Even Leap Year.

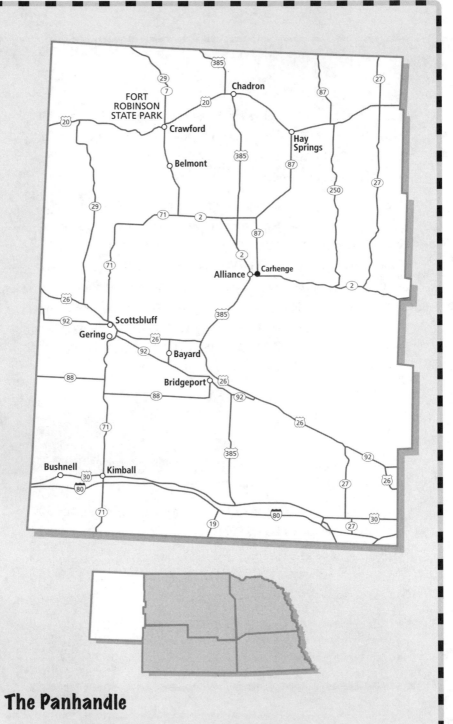

The Panhandle

6

The Panhandle

*T*he farther one is from Nebraska's metro region, the more one hears rumblings of a panhandle secession in order to connect it with another state that is more like the panhandle in demographics and outlook. Why not? It would make this big square state a little more geographically square, while only making it a little less big.

NEBRASKA *Rush Hour*

★ ★

Driving two to four hours to Denver for a weekend or major shopping spree makes more sense to many residents than does driving seven to eight hours to Lincoln or Omaha. Traveling is a big part of everyone's life out here and has been for millennia. The driveway from home to the nearest public road can be miles long, and miles can lie between the nearest ranching neighbors, and more miles required for the daily travel to school, and even more miles to travel between schools. Miles and miles of miles and miles, it's been said.

And what does one see? Never mind that Montana calls itself the Big Sky Country; it has skyspace eaten up by mountains. Out here one never need look up to find the horizon line where sky meets earth, only outward, ever outward.

To those in more populated areas of the country, this wealth of emptiness is a curiosity, and those who choose to reside here even curiouser. A regional cultural event horizon looms palpably from each conversation, newspaper, and radio broadcast; any local colloquialisms are unlikely to escape into the national culture while visiting national aphorisms are tied down by the fabric of local time and space.

It's a big land of big-hearted people who are glad to stop and visit with new acquaintances. Time doesn't pass here so much as it circles 'round again. This was once a land of bison: Herds that dwindled to almost nothing are growing in size and economic importance. Not so long ago, another circle began that is now closing: The Cold War created jobs by digging hundreds of high-tech holes in the ground, offering an odd hunt for a treasure of national security by way of mutually assured destruction. Now these holes are mostly filled in, but vestiges remain in both landscape and mindscape.

The discussion of secession may never go away but simply circle 'round every so often, like some distant cultural moon to the rest of the state.

★ ★

Unhenged
Alliance

Way out west, far from any natural geographic disturbance, in what could be any point of the high plains no different from any other, awash in waves of grain, on the floor of the atmospheric ocean, you're looking for something to rescue you from the monotony. And there it sits—Carhenge, a brilliant example of what can happen to a family reunion that has the right mix of alcohol and heavy machinery.

As the story goes, the instigator had long been a Stonehenge fan. When his family gathered to observe the passing of a patriarch, this inspired artist suggested a memorial, something celebrating the meeting of heaven and earth. The family agreed, and three years later, they met again, brandishing a suitable vision and some serious

"Take care of the moments, the years will take care of themselves." —Maria Edgeworth

★ ★

construction equipment necessary to erect the artwork. Carhenge was dedicated in 1987.

At first the folks in Alliance were bewildered and a tad suspicious. Local authorities had to work through the land-use violations that classified it as a junkyard. Over time, a steadily growing stream of tourists convinced the local business community of the true genius in this work of car art. They grew to appreciate their local visionary artists, kindred to others lionized by the Grassroots Art Center of Lucas, Kansas. Now Stonehenge/Carhenge knockoffs can be found in many states, including Washington, Georgia, Texas, New Mexico, and New Hampshire.

At one point, the display board at the park included pictures from several local businesses that put their own Stonehenge derivative sculptures on display—the shoe store arranged shoe boxes for "Shoe-henge"; the grocery store had something, too—was it "Spamhenge"?

Carhenge has the company of several other sculptures in what is now called the Car Art Reserve. The first addition was of a breeching salmon. The Ford Seasons was another.

Enjoy your visit; while you are driving the long road back home, you can use the time to plan what you'll do at your next family reunion.

Carhenge and the Car Art Reserve are located at 2141 County Road 59. It's open all day, every day, and donations are accepted. For more information, call (800) 738-0648 or go to www.carhenge.com.

Western Pillar
Bayard

If there is an historic case to be made for selecting Nebraska as the most priapic of these United States (isn't there a booth at some national association of Convention and Visitors Bureaus convention with support material for measuring just how priapic your local village or burg might be?), then certainly Chimney Rock catapults Nebraska to the top of consideration.

How Do You Spell Relief?

It's a long way to Carhenge, no matter where you start. It wasn't until very recently that a gift shop was opened on-site, and it's not open all the time. You may need to use the services that just aren't readily available.

Lucky for you that you have this book and know of the rest stop just north of Carhenge about 2 miles, on the east side of the road.

Heed the call.

★ ★

Stalking the original "Penis of the Plains."
Scotts Bluff County Tourism and www.VisitScottsBluff.com

The chimney currently juts 120 feet above the 205-foot base; the base alone provides a vertical topological variation unusual on the mostly flat horizon. Historical comments indicate that the column has worn down over the years. Plenty of historical comments exist to choose from; this erect rock marked a halfway point for many travelers along the Oregon Trail and was mentioned in many pioneer logs. The eroding forces of wind and weather will eventually wear it to a nubbin, but when in view, one can imagine how the lofty spire lifted the spirits of the early travelers trudging across the plains.

Noticeable geologic formations provided landmarks long before the pioneers made it to the plains. Before Europeans arrived, the natives had tagged this prominent protrusion *Heh^aka Che*, or Elk Penis. Imagine the directions: "Go upriver until you get to the big stone Elk Penis, then head north . . . " Undoubtedly the more prim and pious pioneers eschewed the nickname, but cholera, bad weather, and skirmishes demanded more of their attention. It's more likely that schoolmarms, church ladies, and other inventions of polite society insisted on calling this unique geographic signpost Chimney Rock. Cartographers and traveling journalists knew that editors would balk at naughty place names and were glad to pass along terms more palatable to the readers back on the coast.

Tail Tale

Many states endured a kerfuffle about which image to choose for their version of the state quarter. Nebraska had over 6,000 suggestions and narrowed them down to four: Chimney Rock, the State Capitol Building, the Sower, and Chief Standing Bear. It ended up choosing an artist's rendering of pioneers trekking past Chimney Rock. While giving a nod to the importance of this historic landmark, the artist forgot that the chimney has a distinctive look from different sides. As depicted on the quarter, the pioneer wagon representing the westward migration is actually heading east.

Some suggest this was done in a deliberate attempt to better market the state. Think about it. If the state is making a decision about an image that will be circulated nationally, collected by approximately 140 million Americans, and left under an untold number of pillows by tooth fairies—is the best message to have on it one of people working hard to leave the state?

At least they didn't choose a husk of corn.

Which way?

★ ★

Whether recognized or not, it seems clear that the geometry of this rock has influenced much of the man-made buildings and monuments in Nebraska—from the State Capitol to the Woodman Tower to Massacre Canyon Monument. Despite the popularity of male-bashing today, you can't deny the power of the spire to inspire.

Dimensional Travel

Belmont

Englishman Edwin Abbott Abbott published *Flatland: A Romance of Many Dimensions* in 1884. It provides an amusing satire about the social norms of the day and a wonderful introduction to mathematical concepts of multiple dimensions so useful that a film version of the story was released in 2007.

Abbott introduced the reader to this world with these words:

"I call our world Flatland, not because we call it so, but to make its nature clearer to you, my happy readers . . . "

His Flatland was two-dimensional, as were the Flatlanders who lived there. They couldn't "think outside the box" because a three-dimensional box was inconceivable to their worldview—at most they could be encouraged to "think outside the square."

People who experience Nebraska only by coast-to-coast flyovers or bleary-eyed border-to-border drives on I-80 can be forgiven their view that Nebraska is a living Flatland, pressed between an unyielding earth and enormous sky. Breaking topological stereotypes isn't easy.

But just outside of the onetime town of Belmont lies a cartographic Nebraskan oddity that could force those with Flatland views to broaden their thinking to another dimensional level. It's a railroad tunnel built four years after *Flatland* was published, in 1888. Mention that to even longtime Nebraska residents and you'll stir up a bit of curiosity about a terrain in Nebraska so hilly that it made sense to dig a tunnel.

The tunnel was in service until 1983, when nearby hills were dug out and carted away to make room for track that could carry larger cargo. But the lengthy tunnel is still there and makes for a dandy hike from the nearby road.

It's not particularly easy to find, however. First you have to find Belmont, which is a collection of houses well off to the east of combined NE 2/NE 71 south of Crawford. Travel east on North Belmont Road, go south on Breakneck Road until you get to East Belmont Road, and go east. The tunnel is north of the bridge over the railroad tracks, to the east of the current rails.

It's a different dimension.

It's been a time since there's been a train—I don't see any tracks.

★ ★

Let's Rock, Everybody, Let's Rock
Bridgeport

Local word police will remind passers-through who say it differently that their name for the geological formation is really Jail Rock and insinuate that while in town you should call it that, too. If you check the April 1973 listing on the Nebraska Register of National Historic Sites, you'll find an acceptable term of record is Jailhouse Rock.

Like Mother always said, "This is where people end up when they drop out of Schoolhouse Rock." U.S. Geological Survey Photographic Library

A Welcome Sign

Walmart greeters provide an iconic welcome to the millions of shoppers who travel to the stores. A familiar icon provides an unexpected welcome to I-80 travelers who enter Nebraska from the west. It's as though visitors driving down from the very high plains of Wyoming to the not-so-high plains of western Nebraska might need a spiritual cleansing prior to descending any farther—somewhat like saying a prayer before facing an arduous test. Well, that's one possible explanation.

Sculptural billboard welcomes I-80 travelers to Nebraska.

Another could be that it provides a cross-cultural mash-up; a sort of geopolitical mezuzah for the transcontinental drivers entering the western door of Nebraska.

The 180-ton concrete statue rises approximately 40 feet from ground to crown. The statue keeps its back turned on Nebraska, apparently shunning the heart of Husker Nation or confident that westward travelers leaving the state don't need the reassurance of the Blessed Virgin.

The statue is just north of I-80 prior to exit 1, 7 miles west of Bushnell.

★ ★

One point of historical significance of these rocks is that visitors moving west along the Oregon Trail were so intrigued by this protrusion onto the prairie that they would break off from the trail to take a 6- to 8-mile side trip to visit the formation that looked from a distance like a castle or large county courthouse. When was the last time you or someone you know walked that far out of their way to slake their curiosity?

Before you visit, you should decide what you will call these two prominent buttes. No one is suggesting that the insistence on Jail Rock was a local schoolmarm's aversion to a name associated with an Elvis song that was number 1 in both the United States and the United Kingdom and listed by both *Rolling Stone* and the Rock and Roll Hall of Fame as one of the top 500 most important rock songs of all time. Nope, no one is suggesting that at all.

The turnoff west to the geological formation is not quite 5 miles from downtown Bridgeport on NE 88. If you get to the Courthouse and Jail Rock Golf Club (what is "rock golf"?), you've gone too far.

Ain't No Mountain High Enough
Bushnell

Finding the highest point in Nebraska just takes a little common sense. It's the same kind of horse sense you use when you're trying to figure out where the state's lowest point might be. Well, just follow the state's largest river (the Missouri) to the spot where it dumps Omaha's effluent into the luckless neighboring jurisdictions of Kansas and Missouri.

The same is true in your search for the highest peak in corn country. Head west, and when you get as close to Denver as possible, you're teetering at the top of Nebraska. Common sense will get you there; however, it requires a real effort of the imagination to believe that you have arrived at the state's 5,424-foot peak, because Nebraska hasn't wasted any of its geological energy on land forms that jut skyward (Chimney Rock is one of few exceptions to this rule). The state's tallest point is nothing more than a gently rolling field.

I'm on top of the world, Ma!

In typical Midwestern fashion, our indisputable champion of elevation prefers not to call much attention to itself. No Six Flags clutter or Bosselman's mega-gas station here. Not even a state wayside to commemorate this tall achievement in a state short on altitude (but high on attitude!). Nope, you've got to follow the bullet-riddled signs along miles of country roads until a break in the barbed wire allows you to follow tire tracks a short distance to "Panorama Point."

The spot is memorialized with a simple plaque on a pedestal. Chances are you'll have to negotiate past a buffalo or two and a large population of buffalo pies underfoot to reach this pinnacle. The view is suggestive of promising things ahead. The Rocky Mountains hang like rumors on the western horizon, and directly south across the border a herd of wind generators animate the plains, harvesting winds that remain untouched over here.

To find Panorama Point, exit I-80 at the Bushnell exit and head south 10 miles, then 4 miles west, 1 mile south, 2 miles west, and 2 more south.

Walking Among Giants in the Land of the Lost

Chimney Rock and Courthouse Rock illustrate how the brain works, relating personal experiences to familiar metaphors of personal experience; in these cases, the new world culture thought local rock outcropping silhouettes looked like buildings. Artists represent a different way of thinking and seeing that others get to see once they rework raw materials of wood or stone into images that most would not have seen without their touch.

At one point a nationally renowned artist advocated a vision for transforming multiple smaller butte remnants and oversize prairie protuberances around Chadron into multiple monuments to the Sioux Nation. The artist (and onetime Nebraska resident), Gutzon Borglum, whose vision was realized 75 miles to the north in Mount Rushmore, had the idea. Borglum was an artist who liked large-scale projects and American themes; he suggested sculpting an entire tribe of 14-foot to 16-foot sculptures out of multiple existing stone outcroppings in this part of the state.

He died before he could transform his vision into a funded project. Too bad about that. If someone were to try to make his dream a reality today, they'd surely use fiberglass, add some theme park rides or a casino, and then cross-market the sculptures as Happy Meal action figures.

The Horse Thief Whose Horse Let Him Down
Chadron

Like a lot of good ideas, the 1893 Chadron-to-Chicago Cowboy Horse Race started out as a joke. Liquor was probably involved, and nobody could quite recall whose idea it was . . . until it turned out to be a big hit, then everybody claimed it.

★ ★

The year was notable for a financial panic and a world's fair, the Columbian Exposition in Chicago. Buffalo Bill Cody had set up his Wild West Show on the edge of the Exposition grounds. He liked things big and bold, so he promoted the 1,000-mile race and threw in some prize money in exchange for locating the finish line at the entrance to his Wild West arena.

On June 13, a motley assortment of contestants lined up in front of Chadron's Blaine Hotel for the longest horse race in American history. The lineup included Doc Middleton, a recovering horse thief and notorious Nebraska outlaw. Doc had often raced across the state in his thieving days, hotly pursued by angry Sioux Indians or ranchers who wanted their horses and his hide.

Doc's competition included cowpunchers with names like "Rattlesnake" and "Cock-eyed Bill," as well as a stagecoach driver and a token Texan. Rumors had spread that a Miss Emma Hutchinson of Denver would fill out the lineup. Miss Hutchinson was a fetching twenty-one-year-old whom the *New York Times* touted as "a daring horsewoman of long experience." It's doubtful her experience included anything like two weeks in the saddle alongside Doc and Cock-eyed Bill, so the young beauty must have opted for some other daring adventure at the last minute.

Three thousand people cheered at the sound of the starting gun. Each contestant was allowed two horses and had to arrive in Chicago on one of them. The route was laid out in secret so that no contestant could devise a plan in advance that would give them some advantage—for example, by hiding a conveyance for the horses and rider along the way. Instead, they were issued a map at the start of the race that had checkpoints along the way through desolate stretches of Nebraska Sand Hills and prairie, across the Missouri River into Iowa's rolling farmland, and on to the expanse of Illinois beyond the Mississippi River.

As soon as the exhausted riders trudged into Chicago two weeks later, there were charges that the winner had an unfair advantage

because he had helped to lay out the secret route (true). Middleton
was accused of riding in a railroad boxcar part of the way (unsubstan-
tiated, but clearly not out of character). It didn't matter, because both
of Middleton's horses came up lame by the time he reached western
Illinois. The crowd favorite, who had won innumerable races with the
law earlier in life, placed last and went home under a fitting cloud of
disgrace.

Call It Like You See It
Chadron

Driving west on US 20 on the way to Chadron, you find yourself musing about the beauty of these high plains. As you drive along, you
count yourself lucky to be this far off the beaten path, imagining for a
moment or two what it might be like to live on a small, semi-secluded
ranch in these wide-open spaces. You picture a posse of singing cowboys gathering round the bunkhouse with you living the dream of the
American West; all it would take is a little money and some work.

If you are actually watching the road while musing, you would
notice the sign for the Half-Ass Ranch. An odd name to post out by
the highway, you might think. Do they raise mules? Could it reference
a personal dieting success? Maybe a down payment made possible by
winning a lawsuit tied to a tragic clothing malfunction that happened
at the county carnival?

You'll most likely never find out. The easy dream of riding your
horse while driving off into the sunset is more fun than calculating
the actual work it takes to maintain a ranch. Better to leave it at that.

A Census Censorship
Crawford/Fort Robinson

If you one day get a chance to travel this part of the state, imagine
while you look out your window how many miles long was the line of
900 members of the Oglala Lakota trudging toward surrender on

May 6, 1877. Their leader, Crazy Horse, surrendered a short eleven months after his success at the Battles of Rosebud and of Little Big Horn when it became clear that an exodus northward would create too much hardship on the families. It also symbolized an inevitability of the US government's policy of westward expansion.

Historians may argue about the ethics of such policy, but certainly many Nebraskans still won't; it's hard to get a man to see a fault in something if his paycheck depends on it. The lens of time has an

This marks the spot where Crazy Horse was fatally stabbed with a bayonet.

★ ★

ability to clarify once-predominant viewpoints clouded by nationalism and racism. That same distance grows the respect afforded to the man and those who surrendered for the good of the larger group. Still, there must have been resentment among that group of Crazy Horse's warriors who hadn't been defeated in any battle of the Sioux Wars despite being outnumbered and outgunned.

Curators at more than one museum suggest that a playful, passive-aggressive mood was at work among those who stated their names for census represented by the Crazy Horse Surrender Ledger. While some names are curious for today's reader simply because of cultural differences, others are notable because of their vulgar nature—intended as a nose tweak to the authorities just as assuredly as the act of the elementary school rogues stating their names for a substitute teacher. Other historians suggest that these were simply good-natured earthy nicknames common among friends.

The census ledger contains head-of-household names and provides a more interesting read than the nearby Chadron phone book. In order to illustrate the cultural differences, the nose tweaking, and maybe even the fact that Nebraska has long had cultural priapic influences, here are some names from the Surrender Ledger: Fat Rump, Skunk Guts, Big Belly Mule, Scabby Face, One Teet, Tanned Nuts, and Butt Horn. The names only get more obscene from there.

You can take a look at the complete Crazy Horse Surrender Ledger in a 1994 book of the same name held in many libraries and sold in museums in the region (*The Crazy Horse Surrender Ledger*, edited by Thomas Bueker and R. Eli Paul, Nebraska State Historical Society, Lincoln). The original ledger is held by the Nebraska State Historical Society.

Just remember that the lessons of history depend largely on the times in which they were written.

Wrapped in the Flag
Crawford

"Let's paint the house!"

"What, just like that? I can't get you to put a new toilet paper roll on the empty spool or put your tools away and suddenly you've got the time and energy to paint the house? How does that work?"

"It's called division of labor. Plato talked about it. What do you say we do something different this time? Something other than white?"

"Uh-huh. Your division gives me a splitting headache. So, what color did you have in mind? Something adventurous, I'll wager, like beige? Taupe? Sandstone? Camel? Cream?"

Horizontal stripes make you look taller.

"Oh, I don't know. We're in the reddest part of a red state in the middle of the reddest part of the country, and Husker fans to boot. Maybe something in red."

"Red! All of it? All red? Every bit?"

"Sure. It will match the color of the truck out front. If we're going to do something different, we might as well do it up right."

"I'm just not sure that this is 'right.'"

"You're just being timid."

"Am I? Have you thought of using more than one color, maybe even a pattern?"

"You mean like paisley?"

"Sure, if you think you could pull it off, you old hippie. No, I was thinking maybe something like a checkerboard of red and white."

"That could take awhile. And if you have checkerboard-size squares, wouldn't that look more like a pink from the road? I don't want to live in a pink house."

"We could do big squares—three feet per side."

"That wouldn't take as long as checkerboard-size squares, but it would still take longer than one color for everything."

"You've got a point. Stripes? We could do stripes. Like a candy cane."

"Hmm. I like stripes. We could even add a field of stars on a corner of blue."

"Now you're talking with patriotic fervor!"

"So we're agreed. I wonder what the paint job will do to our valuation."

"It's hard to say. But when you are pondering that in your favorite thinking spot, please remember to put a new roll on the spool."

There's no telling how the decision was made. How do you think it happened?

What's That There?

In this part of the world, it's a little hard to find something worthy of the biggest, smallest, or only-est title. Luckily for those who look for such things, the curators at the Wyo-Braska Natural History Museum (aka "Wildlife World") in Gering are quick to point out that they have in their collection the only full-size baluchithere (pronounced buh-loo'-kuh-thir) replica in the world.

"What," you may ask, "is a baluchithere?" It would be tempting to reply with an "Oh, I don't know; about the same as a Baluka anywhere" quip reminiscent of the "About three pounds" answer to the query "What's a henway?" But that won't happen here.

Their baluchithere is a museum-quality replica of the largest land mammal ever to walk the earth, a hornless rhino. And it's the only one around, giving it rights to both the only-est and the biggest of something.

The story of how the display of this prehistoric Pakistani animal came to reside in Gering is a bit unclear. Evidently, this baluchithere is an updated version of one that used to reside in a Lincoln museum; that one there had to be "put down" because it contained asbestos.

It's a big one, Jim. People around there call the 19-foot-tall and 30-foot-long replica Ricky the Rhino.

You can find the museum at 950 U Street, next to the railroad crossing in the renovated depot.

★ ★

Monstrous Development
Hay Springs

Imagine what it takes to be a writer for the local newspaper in a small burg in the middle of Flyover Country. What gets you out of bed in the morning? Is it a nose for news? Maybe it's a community-spirited desire for small-town promotion, or perhaps a penchant to play out the country bumpkin stereotype for naïve big-city editors back East. Newspapers have always looked for ways to increase circulation; outlandish stories have long been a way to drive up readership.

In 1892 the East Coast editors were looking for some exciting news to spice up their local fare. Sensationalism sold papers then as well as it does for end-of-the-checkout-line magazines today. Local writer John G. Maher thought a retelling of an old Native American tale about a water monster seemed like a good idea.

Nessie's got nothin' on this tale.

The first telling was in 1921 in the *Hay Springs News*. Lakeside landowner Arthur Johnson and others were startled to hear and then see a spout of water streaming up 10 to 20 feet from the lake surface. Johnson made as close of an inspection as he dared and described the source as a sea reptile, similar to an alligator, with a rhinolike horn. Stories gathered over the years about how the Alkali Lake Monster would snatch spring calves lost in fog created by its movement in the lake water. As the stories grew, so did the fearsomeness of the beast. It was said to have crawled out onto land to devour a half dozen cows at one sitting, was described more as a giant with green eyes that could spit fire and whose vigorous movement would cause the earth to shake. Size estimates have ranged from 20 feet to an astounding 200 feet long. Alkali Lake, after all, was only a fifty-acre lake.

Newspaper stories went all over the country, and the monster was even written up in *The London Times*, which is purported to have reported that:

"By far the most vivid picture of the actions and features of a medieval monster which for three years has been terrifying the natives of the vicinity of Alkali Lake near the small town of Hay Springs, Nebraska, U.S.A., was received by our Omaha, Nebraska correspondent, today."

About the same time that the Alkali Lake Monster stories were making news, the locals were working on a scheme to make money from curiosity seekers who would pay for the chance to see the monster. They settled on a pay-to-view lake-dragging operation but couldn't negotiate a workable fee with the lakefront property owners.

So a coherent monster capture plan never formed, and international interest in the monster waned. The lake's name was changed from Alkali to Walgren and eventually became part of a state recreation area. But the Lake Monster stories "have legs" even today. The stories of the monster have revived whenever calves were lost over the years and whenever nearby Hay Springs has a town celebration.

Or for that matter, whenever a good tale needs to be told at the local tavern.

There's good news for roving cryptozoologists looking to bed down near a monster's lair. A campground is available at Walgren Lake State Recreation Area. The entrance is located by going 2.5 miles east of Hay Springs on US 20 and NE 87, then 3 miles south on Walgren Lake Road.

That's Sensational!

Colonel John G. Maher wrote not only for the Hay Springs paper but also for the Chadron paper and provided stories to James Gordon Bennet's *New York Herald*. He came up with several sensational stories of the time, including a story of British Naval plans to ply upriver in order to attack Nebraska. He even went so far as to fabricate a cement prehistoric man and then planted it near an archaeological dig near the Black Hills. When "discovered" a few days later by the archaeologists, the Petrified Man was hailed as a tremendous discovery and sent on rounds to the World's Fair and many state and local fairs. Maher couldn't stay mute; he eventually took credit for the hoax.

When asked about his penchant for fabricating tales, he explained that:

"The East felt a great interest in the far West with its Indian fighters, its unexplored territory, its bad lands, and wonders of nature. There was a great demand for stories and a few things to write about so, for an inventive mind there was nothing to do but make up the stories."

Gimme Shelter

Kimball

One thing you can say about Department of Defense spending during the era of MAD (mutually assured destruction): Heightened public panic and fear along with an increasingly sophisticated military-industrial complex left behind a unique infrastructure of architectural properties, the Atlas Inter-Continental Ballistic Missile (ICBM) launch sites.

Many of these sites have been destroyed as part of subsequent arms treaty agreements, but a few remain. Some of the Atlas F series underground silos exist; they look as though someone took one big round grain silo you see in every town around here, turned it upside down and shoved it into the ground, then filled the 50-foot diameter, 175-foot-deep hole with a nuclear-warhead-equipped missile.

The Atlas E series operated a little bit differently from these vertical silos. In the Atlas E configuration, the missile was laid at rest in a horizontal underground position. When signals indicated a need to move from rest to ready, the building ceiling would slowly slide open and the missile would tilt upward into the firing position.

Only twenty-seven of the "coffin launchers" were built. Because of the size of the underground facilities (approximately 19,000 square feet) and the fact that they were built thick and hardened enough to withstand a nearby one-megaton nuclear air blast, the building alone cost roughly $3.5 million to build (in 1960 dollars).

Obviously, if you are in the market for a home that offers you the space of a community recreation center along with the security to defend against a Hollywood-scale zombie invasion, one of these places is for you. And if you want to live in Nebraska on top of that, there's only one.

That one has already been turned into the home of Don and Charlene Zwonitzer on the outskirts of Kimball. They live in the state's biggest private bomb shelter—presumably the only one larger in the state is at Offutt Air Force Base housing some part of StratCom.

★ ★

The Zwonitzers are justifiably proud of the hominess they have built into their Atlas E missile site. They have put a high level of effort into living belowground, creating a multistory greenhouse in the former blast room and installing renewable energy production along with backup diesel generators along with several design touches that look as though they were lifted from a *Midwest Living* pictorial essay.

The Zwonitzers make no secret of the fact that they are worried about the future state of the world. Their home provides them with both a daily safe haven and a sanctuary for troubled times ahead whether those times are caused by seasonal weather phenomena or by social upheaval and civil unrest. It is their cautionary view that makes them eager to share their example to any who are curious about what it might be like to live in an apocalyptic time.

There's no place like this home!

⋆ ⋆

For many westbound I-80 travelers, this remote part of the road seems end of the world enough. But if your and their schedules permit, it's worth the time to share pointers on dealing with doom.

The Zwonitzers' home is south of the Kimball exit (number 20) on NE 71. You can reach the Zwonitzers by calling (308) 235-2708.

Steeple Chase
Scottsbluff

In an era when television decorating, reconstruction, or makeover shows serve as thirty-minute commercials operating under the guise of design advice, it's worth noting that how one chooses to decorate the outside of one's home is a public expression of personal definition and character.

The enthusiastic yard decorator occasionally enjoys a bit of whimsical peek-a-boo in an otherwise ordinary landscape. Real estate developers have done their best to replicate the Levittown tract housing conventionality building model; yard art can break the monotony.

Oft-found yard decorations that counter the local repetitiveness of the Husker logo iconography include kitschy plastic deer, painted plywood gardener's bums, antique farm implements, or a cowboy silhouette.

For some, the whimsy can become overwhelming—either by overuse on the part of one homeowner or due to faddish purchasing decisions in a neighborhood. When that happens, local good-taste police occasionally create and enforce neighborhood covenants. Even when such rules apply, vigilantes and youthful pranksters occasionally "liberate" the characters from their duties in a yard. Garden gnomes are the ones most susceptible to action; the international Garden Gnome Liberation Front has secretive members throughout the world ready to go gnome hunting. Once captured, a gnome is often returned to the wild.

Tucked into a backyard in an older neighborhood in town, one homeowner has chosen to collect something a little out of the ordinary, and large enough to avoid random acts of pilferage. This yard has three church steeples to inspire the owner and passersby. They're from different denominations, or at least different architects. The steeples look like gazebos for genuflecting gardeners more than kitschy ornamentation.

And here is the steeple. And here. And here. Paul McMeekin

index

A

Abbott, Chris, 187

Abbott, Edwin Abbott, 212

Abbott, Ethel, 187

Adamson, Kissin' Jack, 121

African-American farm
community, 175

Akron, 4

Alda, 134–36

Alexander, Grover Cleveland, 194

Alkali Lake Monster, 226–28

Alliance, 207–8

Alma, 136, 138

Anderson, Ike, 17–18

Andy the Footless Goose, 106–8

Arbor Day, 118, 119

Archie the Mammoth, 49–50

Art Chicks—A Girlfriends
Gallery, 112–14

Art Farm, 115–16

Art Harvest, 116

Arthur, 174

Ashburn, Richie, 38

Ashfall Fossil Beds State Historical
Park, 33, 36

assemblage art, 148–50

asteroids, 138–39

Atlas Inter-Continental Ballistic
Missile launch sites, 229–31

Audacious, 175

Aurora, 92–93

Avoca, 93–95

Avoca Duck Races, 93–95

B

Bacon, Kevin, 74

Bailey Yard, 161–64

baluchithere replica, 225

Bar, The, 128–29

Bartak's Depression, 189–91

Bartling brothers, 127–28

bat bombs, 73

Batterton, Lee, 130

Battle Creek, 6–8

Bayard, 208, 210–12

Behlen, Walter, 12–13

Behlen Family and Community
Fallout and Blast-Resistant
Shelters, 13

Behlen Manufacturing Company,
12–13

Bellevue, 96–97

Bellwood, 8–10

Belmont, 212–13

Bennet, 98–99

Big Hill, 199–200

bison, 136, 151–52

Blackbird, Chief, 14–15

Blackbird Hill, 14–15, 17

Blackbird Scenic Overlook, 17

Blagdon, Emery, 197–98

Bock's Car, 74

body piercings, 88

bombing, 36–37

bomb shelters, 17–18, 229–31

Boosalis, Helen, 67

Boot Hill, 157–59

index

bordello, 148–50

Borglum, Gutzon, 218

bowling, 52–53

Boys Don't Cry (film), 111–12

Boys Town, 69–70, 72

Bridgeport, 214, 216

Brock, 100–101

Brockman, Ida, 63

Broken Bow, 175–76

Brown, Matt, 87–88

Brownlee, 175

Bryan, William Jennings, 82

Buffett, Warren, 97, 153

Bug Eaters, 49

Burlington Rooms, 150

Bush, George W., 96–97

Bushnell, 216–17

C

Cairo, 176–77

Cambridge, 138–39

capital punishment, 100

Car Art Reserve, 208

Carhenge, 207–8, 209

Carson, Johnny, 29, 30, 108

Carswell, G. Harrold, 81

Catlin, George, 14–15

cattle fallout shelter survival test, first, 17–18

Cattlemen's Restaurant, 196

Cavett, Dick, 29

Cedar County Historical Museum, 23

cemeteries, 117, 119, 161, 182–83

center pivots, 16

Chadron, 218–20

Chadron-to-Chicago Cowboy Horse Race, 218–20

Cherry County, 199–200

Chicago, Burlington & Quincy Railroad Concert Band, 160

Chickendale Dancers, 40–42

"Children of the Corn" (King), 5

Chimney Rock, 62, 208, 210–12

church steeples, 231–32

CliffsNotes, 54

Clinton, Bill, 153–55

clowns, 31–32

Cody, Buffalo Bill, 219

Colon, 10–12

Colossal Colon, 12

Columbus, 12–14

Comstock, 178–79

Comstock Labyrinth, 178–79

Conley Flat Cemetery, 182–83

corn, ix, xi

cornfields, 16

corrugated steel home, 12–13

Cozad, 139–42

Cozad, John, 139–41

Crawford, 220–24

Crazy Horse, 221–22

Crazy Horse Surrender Ledger, 222

index

Crenshaw, Ben, 186
Critter Corral, 197
crop circles, 16

D

Danish Baker, 179–81
Dannebrog, 179
Davisson, Harold, 124–25
Day, Doris, 60
Deaver, Clem, 175
Decatur, 14–15, 17
DeFrain, Dennis, 17–18
DeWitt, 101–2
Dismal River Golf Club, 186
Dorothy Lynch salad
    dressing, 194
Double Piddler, 93
Dundee, 72–73
dwarf mammoth, 50

E

Easterwood, Horace, 175–76
Edgerton, Harold, 93
Edgerton Explorit Center, 93
Eiler, Elsie, 26–27
Electoral College, 55
electric chair, 100
Eli, 182–83
Elkhorn, 17–18
Elkhorn Valley Museum, 30
Endicott, 102–3
Enola Gay, 74
Epler, Stephen, 150

Eppley, Eugene, 82–83
Eppley Airfield, 82–83
ethanol, xi
Exon, James J., 82

F

Fairbury, 104, 106
farm artifacts, 4
Filley, Elijah, 103
Filley Stone Barn, 103
fire balloons, 72–73
fitness, 69
flag-painted house, 223–24
Flatland (Abbott), 212
flat topography, 137
Fleming, Gene, 106–8
food processing, 67–69
football, 49, 55, 134–36,
    150–51
Fort Robinson, 220–22
Foy George Memorial Band
    Shell, 32
Fred (roadhouse proprietor),
    166–68
Fremont, 18–20
Fremont Days, 19
Friend, 105
Friendship Patio, 178–79
Frisbee, 65
Fugate, Caril Ann, 51, 98–99
Funk, 142–43
Funk, P.C., 142
Funk-Odessa Highway, 143

index

G

Gaffin, J.N., 49

Gatlin (fictional town), 5

Gering, 225

Giant Hill, 199–200

Giant Marijuana Forest of
    Eastern Nebraska, 91

Ginsberg, Allen, 57, 59

Glur's Tavern, 14

goldenrod, 63

Goldie (prostitute), 167

governors, 67, 82

Grant County, 188

grasshopper cycles, 103

Great American Desert,
    ix, 16

Great Navy of the State of
    Nebraska, 145

Grotto, 86

Groundhog Day, 128–29

Grover Cleveland Alexander
    Days, 194

H

Half-Ass Ranch, 220

Halsey, 183–85

Halsey National Forest,
    183–85

Hansen, Sandy, 197

Happy Jack Chalk Mine,
    194–95

Hartington, 20, 22–23

Harvard, 106–8

Harvey P. Sutton House,
    159–61

Hastings, 146–50

Hastings Museum of Natural and
    Cultural History, 147

hate crime, 110–12

Hay Springs, 226–28

Healing Machines, 197–98

heavy toddler, 138

Hebron, 108–10

Henri, Robert, 139, 140, 141–42

Hickok, Wild Bill, 102–3

highest point, 200, 216–17

High Plains Aquifer, 144–45

Hildreth, 150–51

History of Nebraska (Olson and
    Naugle), 29

Hooker County, 185–86

horses, 191–93

hot dogs, 104

Hruska, Roman, 81

Hubbard, L. Ron, 37

Hudson, Rock, 60

Humboldt, 110–12

Husker fans, 134–36

Husker Holler, 91

Hutchinson, Emma, 219

Hyannis, 186–88

I

I-80, 137, 143, 153–56, 215

International Quilt Studies Center
    and Museum, 50–51

index

"In the Year 2525 (Exordium and Terminus)" (song), 58
Iowa, 47, 84

J
Jailhouse Rock, 214, 216
Johnny Carson Gallery, 30
Johnson, Arthur, 227
Joslyn Castle, 71

K
Kearney, 151–56
Kearney Arch, 153–56
Kenfield, Harvey, 164–65
Kenfield, Howard, 164–65
Kewpies, 6–8
Kimball, 229–31
King, Stephen, 5, 99
Klein, Marty, 63
Klown Doll Museum, 32
Klown Festival, 32
Kool-Aid, 146–47
Kool-Aid Days, 147

L
Lake Waconda, 111
landlocked states, 21
Larry the Cable Guy, 121
Late Show, 39–40
Lee's Legendary Marble Museum, 130
Leon Myers Stamp Center, 72
Letterman, David, 39–40

Lewis & Clark Corps of Discovery, 1, 3, 25
Liars Hall, 181
Lime Creek Observatory, 138–39
Lincoln, 48–69
Lincoln Industries, 66
Lindbergh, Charles, 187
Lindholm, Robert, 138–39
Liska, Danny, 27–29
Little People, 28–29
Louisville, 112–14
Lover Come Back (movie), 60
Lowell, 157–59
lowest point, 123–24, 216
Loy, Myrna, 191
lumberjack, giant, 8–9
Lynch, 23–25
Lynch, Dorothy, 194

M
Maher, John G., 226, 228
maize, xi
mammoth fossils, 48–50
Mandigo, Roger, 68–69
Manure River, 136, 138
marbles, 129–30
Marquette, 115–16
Martin, Richard, 188–89
Mason City, 188–89
Massacre Canyon, 168–70
McCook, 158, 159–61
McDowell, Nelson, 104, 106

index

McDowell's Tomb, 104, 106
mediocrity, 81
Memorial Stadium, 55
Men's Fitness magazine, 69
Merna, 189–91
Mick, Gerald, 9–10
Middleton, Doc, 219, 220
Midland Co-op, 143
Milford, 114–15
Milgram, Stanley, 75
Missouri River, 47
models, 127–28
Monowi, 25–27
monuments to Sioux Nation,
    proposed, 218
Morrill Stadium, 134–36
Morton, J. Sterling, 118, 119
motorcycle trips, 29
Mullen, 185
mumblety-peg, 22
Mutual Insurance Heritage
    Museum, 7–8

N
Naper, 191–93
Naugle, Ronald C., 29
Nebraska, as term, 137
Nebraska City, 117–19
"Nebraska" (Springsteen),
    51, 99
Nebraska Star Party, 201
Nebraska State Capitol, 61–62
Nebraska State Fair, 59–60

Nebraska Wesleyan University,
    63–65
Nebraskits, 19
Nelson, 119–20
Neuhaus, Gayle, 43–44
Nicholas, Jack, 186
Nichols, George Ward, 102–3
Niobrara, 27–29
Nolte, Nick, 74
Norfolk, 30
Norris, George, 158
North Platte, 161–64
nuclear power plant, small, 20

O
O'Brien, Mr., 4
Odd Museum, 53
officers, general, 76
Offutt Air Force Base, 74,
    96–97
Ogallala, 164–65
Ogallala Lakota, 220–22
Old Baldy, 25
Oldenburg, Claes, 54, 56
Ole's Big Game Steakhouse and
    Lounge, 165–66
Olson, James C., 29
Omaha, 45, 47, 69–88
Omaha Airport Authority, 83
Omaha Public Power
    District, 20
O'Neill, Rose, 6–8
Orr, Kay, 67

index

Osterman, Alice, 193–94
O Street, 57–59
outhouses, vintage, 43–44
Outsider Art, 23–25
Oxbow Pioneer Memorial Park, 9–10
Oxbow Trail, 9

P

palindromes, 85–86
Palmer, Arnold, 30
Palmyra, 121–22
Pandray, George Edward, 126
panhandle secession, 205
Panorama Point, 216–17
Paulson, Arlene, 203
Pavilion Hotel, 199
Pawnee, 168–70
Paxton, 165–66
penknives, 20, 22–23
Pepe's Restaurant, 66
Perkins, Edwin, 146–47
Petersen, Bill, 102
Petrified Man, 228
petrified wood, 183
Petrified Wood Gallery, 164–65
Petro, Marilyn, 65
phrases, notable, 80–81
Pilgrim Holiness Church, 174
Plainview, 31–32
Platte River, 133, 134–36, 137
Podunk, 100–101

police station, smallest, 105
porch swings, 108–10
"Postcards from Nebraska" (television segment), 181
Postmark, Valentine, 203
prairie dogs, 25
Project X-Ray, 73

Q

Quack-Off Races, 95
quarter, state, 61–62, 211

R

railroad tunnel, 212–13
Rat Olympics, 63–65
Ravenscroft, Thurl, 30
Rawhide Creek, 19–20
Red Willow County, 161
Republican River, 136, 138
restroom, second best, 112
rest stop, 209
roadside vendors, 114–15
Robert Henri Museum, 141–42
Roberts Dairy Company, 17–18
Rochelle, Holly, 12
Rocky Mountain oysters, 125–26
"Rollin' to Colon" bicycle tour, 12
Royal, 32–33, 36
Rudy's Library, 25–27
Rulo, 122–24

index

S

Sacramento, 166–68
sale barns, 121–22
sandhill cranes, 133, 134–36
Sand Hills, 171, 183, 199
Sand Hills Golf Club, 186
Sandoz, Mari, ix
Schroeder, Tom, 179–81
Scientology, 37–38
Scotia, 194–95
Scottsbluff, 231–32
sculptures, metal, 65–66,
    188–89
2nd Wind Ranch, 179
Seneca, 195–96
September 11, 2001, 96–97
Serres, Cowboy Joe, 44
Seward, 124–25
Shannon, George, 1, 3
Sheridan County, 199–200
Sioux, 168–70, 218
six degrees of separation,
    74–75
Sonnenfeld, Jeremy, 53
South Bend, 125–26
Sower, The, 61–62
SPAM factory, 18–19
Speakeasy Restaurant, 167–68
speed limit, 111
Springsteen, Bruce, 51, 99
St. Joseph Hospital, 86
St. Paul, 193–94
Standing Bear, 80

Stansbury, William, 120–21
Stansbury building, 120–21
Stapleton, 196–98
Starkweather, Charlie, 51,
    98–100
statue, concrete, 215
Stewart, Dave, 148–50
straw bale construction, 174
strobe lighting, 92–93
Sun Valley Lanes, 53
Sutton, Harvey, 160
Swank, Hilary, 110
Swanson company, 68
Sweet Shoppe, 194

T

Tarnov, 36–37
tavern, old, 14
tax policy, 78–79
Taylor, 198–99
Teena, Brandon, 110–12
Testicle Festival, 126
Thompson, Cal, 192
Thompson, Ruth, 192–93
Thone, Charles, 82
Tilden, 37–38
time capsule, 124–25, 126
time zones, 195–96
To Kill a Mockingbird
    (movie), 108
Tonight Show, The, 108
Tony the Tiger, voice of, 30
tornadoes, 35, 122

index

Torn Notebook (Oldenburg and van Bruggen), 54, 56
town, smallest, 27
Tree City, 117–19
Turner, Ted, 151–53, 186
Two Wheels to Adventure (Liska), 29

U

Unadilla, 127–29
Unadilla Bill, 128–29
Unforgiven (movie), 156
Union Pacific Railroad, 161–64
United States Olympic Committee, 63–64
University of Lincoln, 68–69
University of Nebraska at Omaha, 69, 76
University of Nebraska-Lincoln, 50–51, 54, 55, 91, 134–36
University of Nebraska State Museum of Natural History, 48–50
US Strategic Command (STRATCOM), 96–97

V

Valentine, 200–203
van Bruggen, Coosje, 54, 56
Vise-Grip, 101–2
Vo, Loi, 66
volcanic ash, 32–33, 36

W

Wahoo, 39–40, 105
Walgren Lake State Park, 227–28
Wayne, 40–42
Wayne Chicken Parade, 40–42
Wayne Chicken Show, 40–42
weather, 34–35
Weeder's, 23–25
Weiner Schlinger, 104
Welsch, Roger, 181
Westward Ho Park, 115
White Horse Ranch, 192–93
White Horse Troupe, 192
White Spot of the Nation, 78–79
whittling, 23
"Wichita Vortex Sutra" (Ginsberg), 57, 59
Winnetoon, 43–44
Woods, Grant, 82–83
World's Cleanest Airport, 82
World's Largest Covered Wagon, 115
World's Largest Stamp ball, 69–70, 72
World War II, 72–74
Wright, Frank Lloyd, 159–61
Wuebben, Hugo, 23
Wyo-Braska Natural History Museum, 225
Wyuka Cemetery, 117, 119

index

X

X., Malcolm, 76–78

Xtreme Rat Challenge, 64

Y

yard decorations, 231–32

York, 129–30

Z

Zwonitzer, Charlene, 229–31

Zwonitzer, Don, 229–31

Zybach, Frank, 16

about the authors

David Harding is a journalist, public relations consultant, and book editor and publisher for private clients. He writes a column on Omaha and Nebraska history for the *Omaha World-Herald* and is a partner in Legacy Preservation LLC, which produces family and business histories for clients in Nebraska and elsewhere. He manages press and public information outreach for a regional government in Alaska, where he lived for twenty years. Harding and his wife, Sarah, have three children and live in Omaha.

Rick Yoder has spent his career working on sustainability solutions for businesses, most currently with the University of Nebraska at Omaha where he directs the Pollution Prevention Regional Information Center. His work on energy efficiency, water conservation, and waste reduction has taken him on numerous travels throughout the United States, where he delights in finding the curiosities available there.

Other titles in the Curiosities series

Alabama Curiosities, 2nd
Arizona Curiosities, 2nd
Big Book of New England Curiosities
Colorado Curiosities
Connecticut Curiosities, 2nd
Delaware Curiosities
Florida Curiosities, 2nd
Georgia Curiosities, 2nd
Indiana Curiosities, 3rd
Iowa Curiosities, 2nd
Kansas Curiosities, 2nd
Kentucky Curiosities, 2nd
Maine Curiosities, 2nd
Maryland Curiosities
Massachusetts Curiosities, 2nd
Michigan Curiosities, 2nd
Minnesota Curiosities, 2nd
Missouri Curiosities, 2nd
Nevada Curiosities
New Hampshire Curiosities
New Jersey Curiosities, 2nd
New Mexico Curiosities
New York Curiosities
North Carolina Curiosities
Northern California Curiosities
Ohio Curiosities
Oklahoma Curiosities
Oregon Curiosities
Pennsylvania Curiosities, 3rd
Rhode Island Curiosities
Seattle Curiosities
South Dakota Curiosities
Southern California Curiosities
Texas Curiosities, 3rd
Utah Curiosities
Vermont Curiosities
Virginia Curiosities, 2nd
Washington Curiosities, 2nd
Wisconsin Curiosities, 3rd
Wyoming Curiosities